PORTER'S SECRET

FITZ JOHN PORTER'S MONUMENT DECODED

by

WAYNE SOINI

JETTY HOUSE
an imprint of PETER E. RANDALL PUBLISHER
Portsmouth, New Hampshire
2011

ISBN: 978-0-9828236-8-2

Library of Congress Control Number: 2011931831

Published by:
Jetty House
an imprint of
Peter E. Randall Publisher
P.O. Box 4726
Portsmouth, NH 03802

www.perpublisher.com

Book design:
Grace Peirce
www.nhmuse.com

All original photographs are by Doug Kerr, dmkerr@dmkerr.com

Dedicated to my mother,
Florence M. Soini,
who gave me my first history book.

Contents

"I hear constantly of taking strong positions and holding them, of lines of retreat and of bases of supplies. Let us discard such ideas."
>—John Pope, Major General, greeting the Army of Virginia upon assuming command,
>>(July 14, 1862)

"What shall I do?"
>—Fitz John Porter, Major General, Corps commander, Fifth Corps, Army of the Potomac, shouting after General McDowell as McDowell rode off during Second Bull Run,
>>(August 29, 1862)

"This day of the 29th, which is among his proudest, will stand in history as one of his wisest and best days."
>—Joseph Choate, America's premiere trial lawyer, who represented General Porter before the Schofield board, speaking of Porter on August 29, 1862 in his closing argument,
>>(January 11, 1879)

Preface

Dead men tell no tales.

Unless they leave a monument.

General Fitz John Porter's monument at Haven Park in his native Portsmouth, New Hampshire, is a tale told by an equestrian statue, three bronze *bas reliefs* and one long paragraph tablet. The monument's artwork, as if it were in code, explores and explains a historical mystery. Between its lines and images, Porter's monument is an eyewitness account of disobedience in battle. Working with a sculptor, Porter made his side public here for all time.

Porter, whose name may mean nothing to the casual visitor to Haven Park, is the Civil War scholars' Rorschach Test. Porter at Second Bull Run is their White Whale. Porter's name is a fighting word among academics who heatedly debate whether to place Porter among the good guys, the bad guys or the mere klutzes of the Civil War. The battle of words has lasted many times the length of the Civil War. Wallace J. Schutz and Walter N. Trenerry, who co-authored *Abandoned by Lincoln, A Military Biography of General John Pope*, rightly wrote that the cause of the Union disaster at "the Second Battle of Bull Run was fought and refought in the Oval Office, before a general court-martial, before a Board of Review, in hot and nasty letters to and from survivors, in newspapers and magazines, in the smoke-filled chambers of party caucuses, in the committee rooms and on the floor of the House and Senate, in lecture halls, in history books." Porter intended a visitor to Haven Park to stand beside him in this controversy, to see it through his eyes, and to support him. His tale is of a man who refused to order his men to their deaths for no purpose at the center of the Second Battle of Bull Run.

The drama of Porter versus his commander at Second Bull Run, General John Pope, rides again in Portsmouth. Astonishingly, even after Porter's court-martial and a 38-day hearing with 142 witnesses before a Presidential commission, basic questions remain unanswered about one of the most written-about wartime events, itself the most notorious three-day battle of the war, the greatest Union defeat, Lee's greatest victory—in his book, *Return to Bull Run; The Campaign And Battle of Second Manassas*, John J. Hennessy, the dean of scholars of Second Bull Run, wrote that "before 1890 probably no battle, including Gettysburg, received more attention" That this battle is re-enacted in a Portsmouth park in stone and bronze is no wonder.

Porter's ornate Victorian monument presents no traditional tribute to a military hero but is, instead, a man's answer to everybody, to the charges of his persecutors and to the doubts of his friends as well. For example, his friend, General James Harrison Wilson thought that Porter's behavior at the Battle of Malvern Hill was "most credible if not glorious," but Wilson wondered aloud all of his life "what it was that paralyzed him in the Pope Campaign." Porter's inaction during Second Bull Run on August 29, 1862, is explained in his monument by implication. Second Bull Run, not named on the front tablet, and Porter's disobedience to General Pope's orders, nowhere directly depicted, are illuminated nonetheless by clues hidden in plain sight.

Porter was simply the sanest Civil War general on either side and, at Second Bull Run, it got him into trouble. The unquestioned hero of several other battles, Porter did not crack at Second Bull Run; nor did he crack when he was thrown out of the Army in disgrace in 1863 for his inaction under fire and disobedience to orders at Second Bull Run. He struggled hard to be heard until, seventeen years after Second Bull Run, the Army's top three generals realized that Porter was right and the court-martial was wrong. They found that Porter judged what was going on, acted correctly, and rightly disobeyed his commander, General Pope. The three generals, including the head of the Army General John Schofield (all war veterans), unanimously voted to exonerate Porter. Following their recommendation, Congress and the President restored Porter's civil rights and wartime rank and benefits in 1886.

One grasps that Porter's story is unusual. So is Porter's monument. Porter had the opportunity to decide how he would be remembered because he outlived his cousin. Robert H. Eddy, a rich patent attorney and Porter's New Hampshire-born cousin, left $30,000 in his will, the equivalent today of a quarter-million dollars, for the creation of the greatest privately-funded Civil War memorial ever constructed. With price no object, Porter arranged for the country's most prominent Civil War monument designer, James E. Kelly, to execute the project. Porter could and did work closely with Kelly at the sculptor's Manhattan studio and at Porter's house in nearby Montclair, New Jersey.

Reminiscences

of a

Life in Peace and in War—

—of peace in War and war in peace.

The Autobiography

of

Fitz John Porter.

Late Colonel of the U. S. Army
and
Major General of Volunteers.

and

For more than twenty years

suffering under an Unjust Stigma

inflicted and maintained by his Government

If Porter had completed his autobiography, including his own detailed explanation of the thinking behind his controversial decisions during the Second Battle of Bull Run, he and Kelly may not have designed a monument of clues to be decoded that sheds light on August 29, 1862. (Photo courtesy of the Library of Congress; James Erik, http:// JamesErik.com.)

Close cooperation was necessary as the two men raced against time. Although Porter died in 1901, the monument's design was only final on Thanksgiving Day, 1900. So sick that day that he stayed in his bed, diabetic Porter, his kidneys failing, upstairs, approved the equestrian statue. Kelly, downstairs with the family, used his chance and on that festive day sagely laid out sketches of three tablets before the family. After everybody was stuffed, the happy, sleepy family sparred only a bit. Porter's oldest and smartest son, Holbrook, an inventor whom Porter designated in his will to defend his memory, had an idea. Holbrook demanded that the name of a belated supporter of his father, GENERAL GRANT, be included. There was some concern. After all, General Grant had not been at Second Bull Run. Grant was finally included not as an eyewitness but as an expert witness. Accordingly, in bold letters on front of the monument, Holbrook's suggestion on that Thanksgiving Day in Montclair, bears fruit in Portsmouth to this day. The name of GENERAL GRANT, the last ally to join Porter's cause, appears in raised letters. As certainly intended, GENERAL GRANT's approval of Porter impresses visitors much like the *Good Housekeeping* Seal of Approval. With the wording of the front tablet complete, the statue and Kelly's three *bas reliefs* agreed, all details of the complex monument were set in Porter's lifetime.

Kelly had no Civil War secrets or stories of his own to tell. A non-veteran, Kelly as a young boy in Brooklyn had only seen troops, their rifles on their shoulders, march off to war in their blue uniforms while officers with golden swords at their side rode by on splendid horses. Kelly's boyhood fascination with the war intensified as he grew older. The self-taught sculptor made memorialization of the Civil War into his life's work. Kelly's statue of General John Buford still stands at Gettysburg, his "Sheridan's Ride" is in a national museum, his Civil War Soldiers and Sailors Monument in Yonkers spectacularly commemorates New York's veterans, and other bronze statues and busts embody the Civil War across the country. For Kelly's largest one-man monument, his subject chose the scenes that his monument would depict, determined the wording of the front tablet, and reviewed, revised and finally approved Kelly's equestrian model.

Cracking Porter's and Kelly's code requires a visitor to notice the unexpected omission of Second Bull Run, to analyze the monument's three surprising images of war, and to study the tightly-woven words on the front of the monument. With such scrutiny and analysis, a window opens on the controversy that swept Porter out of the Army in disgrace; the same episode that historians find difficult to understand, the mystery of Porter's inaction that made General Wilson always wonder, although an event nowhere directly presented on Porter's monument.

The monument does not boast that Porter's inaction saved General Pope's entire army from destruction, although Porter's inaction most certainly did. Porter may literally have saved the Union itself when one considers that, over the dead bodies of Pope's army, a successful invasion and capture of Washington by General Robert E. Lee could well have followed Second Bull Run. In that case, there would have been no Antietam. And there would have been no Emancipation Proclamation. And cotton-starved England and emboldened France might then have intervened in the American civil war on the Confederate side. That nightmare's likelihood, of rebels marching into Washington and the stars and bars flying over the Capitol, is for each reader of this book or visitor to Porter's monument to work out to his or her own satisfaction. It is a plausible, if not compelling, scenario. But even limited to the impact on the single day of August 29, 1862, when Porter at least saved his own ten-thousand men, the story of the monument in Portsmouth is one that every American should know.

A note on punctuation and spelling: This is not a scholarly treatise. I have eschewed brackets for inserted or modified words and likewise omitted the ellipses that traditionally signal words omitted from quotations. Without any trace of having done so, I have changed pronouns from first- to third-person or substituted names for pronouns, and vice versa. I have also corrected or added punctuation silently, inserted conjunctions or bridge words, and modernized spelling. I made these reader-friendly simplifications in order that the average reader might assimilate each speaker or author with greater ease. A Bibliography is appended.

A note on sources: I list all of my sources in the Bibliography. In the Acknowledgements section and occasionally also in the text of this book, I express my gratitude for sources that were especially useful. I do not mean to suggest that any one or all of them would agree with the inferences or conclusions I present in this book! On the contrary, I believe that the authors of the sources would disagree with my analysis of official records and my radical reading of Porter's monument. I probably stand alone—unless I am right, in which case I proudly stand alongside General Fitz John Porter.

—Wayne Soini

Enigmatic Fitz John Porter was determined to leave behind selected images of himself and of his military career that would defend his reputation. The image of himself passing in review, saluting the colors, his face set and determined (as they are in wartime photos of Porter in the field) was intended to emphasize his patriotism and to plead "Not Guilty!" to charges of which he was convicted by court-martial in January, 1863. (Photo courtesy of Doug Kerr)

1

The Deceptive Statue

The straightforwardness suggested by the monument's larger-than-life statue of General Fitz John Porter on horseback, in uniform, eyes front, head uncovered, holding his Union cap over his heart, saluting the flag, is deceptive.

Superficially, it is a realistic image of great precision, the product of a sculptor who was able to study his subject up close and at length. James E. Kelly first met Porter in New York, finding him at work on an upper floor of the main post office, where Porter occupied a small, quiet office away from the loading docks and customers for stamps and where Porter greeted Kelly heartily. Before the Civil War, Porter withstood the rigors of the field in Kansas and Utah, then places where living conditions wavered between survival and civilization-in-progress. During the Civil War, Porter fought despite fevers and chills and extreme fatigue. During his most serious illness, dysentery in mid-August, 1862, he continued to generate orders, dispatches and letters. He rode, camped and fought with his Fifth Corps and never once yielded his command. However, Kelly arrived just in time, as the well-preserved slim, trim Porter's robust constitution was about to fail him. The artist, who never married and had no family to distract him from his work, shuttled frequently back and forth by trolley between his studio in New York and Porter's home in Montclair, where he sketched Porter posing with strings for reins, quizzed him about riding technique, and even made notes about the manner in which his boots touched the stirrups. Thanks to William B. Styple's award-winning *Generals in Bronze*, published in 2005, we can literally eavesdrop on

Porter and Kelly as they worked together. In Porter's opinion—and he was fastidious about accuracy—and in his wife's opinion, the statue mirrored him during the Civil War.

Porter was not the only one to think so.

When Union General Joshua Chamberlain saw the statue atop the monument in Portsmouth, he saw the Porter that he had known during the war. Famous as the Bowdoin professor who commanded Maine troops at Gettysburg, Chamberlain wrote to Kelly soon after Porter's monument was unveiled. He told Kelly that the artist showed Porter exactly "as I used to see him at the head of his corps in 1862." Kelly, Chamberlain said, had rendered service "not only to General Porter's friends but to the truth of history."

General Chamberlain was more right than he ever knew. The Porter monument was designed *in toto* to serve the truth of history. Below the statue a connect-the-dots narrative is offered from which to see a historical truth. Our first clue comes from looking very closely at Porter's statue. The shoulders-back equestrian figure at the top of the monument resembles many other statues of many other generals in many other parks. Porter and his family thought that it was he to the life, as did General Chamberlain. But Kelly was crafty. An artist juggles symbols as a juggler juggles balls. Working by implication, with symbols, Kelly stated the issue, which was of the general's state of mind. The statue of General Porter holding his Union cap over his heart asks the questions:

Why did Porter fail to charge the enemy as ordered by General Pope on August 29, 1862?

What was in his heart?

Porter's focused stare at his country's flag is a counterpoint to his court-martial.

Kelly and Porter argued over the regulation salute. Kelly, who had often had top officers of the Union pose and salute for him, and Porter, who knew how he had saluted, both had a basis for their conclusion. Kelly preserved the almost-goofy dialogue of an artist arguing with a general over how to salute in a brief, undated note now at the New York Historical Society, one of a handful of Kelly's notes that were not published in Styple's great book:

"Kelly: I want to represent you saluting the colors.

"I stood up and showed him the action.

"Kelly: Do you remember it?

"Porter: I don't remember it. We generally did this way making a salute."

Kelly had the last word on using the salute pose but, gesturing hand over heart, Porter had the last gesture. Kelly's saluting figure, head bared as if in the presence of God, with open, unblinking eyes staring straight ahead at the flag, Union cap over the heart, suggests zealous and unbending patriotism. Porter's statue pleads "Not Guilty." Moreover, other pieces of the puzzle from which to reconstruct Porter's state of mind at Second Bull Run on the day of his disobedience adorn Porter's monument under the statue. Through the monument's statue, its three *bas reliefs* and its large front panel, one may infer Porter's inmost secret. That secret circles endlessly, night and day, in Haven Park, from the flag-saluting statue on down.

The saluting, ramrod-backed, uniform-clad, solemn-faced rider is deceptive on its surface in one other way. Kelly wanted to portray Porter not as stiff but as serene. True, Porter sometimes seemed like a statue. True, Porter's admiring fellow Union general, General Thomas "Meagher of the Sword" Meagher, described Porter in battle in his official report as a "stone wall." (By the time Meagher said it, that nickname had

Fitz John Porter, circa. 1862. (Photo courtesy of the Library of Congress; James Erik, http://JamesErik.com.)

already been taken or "Stonewall" might have been a Union general.) But the longest verbal portrait of Porter during the war, which shows him animated, alert and in good spirits above all others of his rank, came from the pen of General George B. McClellan. Written at a time of terrible struggle following disappointing reverses that stung him to the core, McClellan wrote his wife that Porter was "all that I thought him & more. Nothing has depressed him; he is always cheerful, active & ready, & is much more efficient than all put together." Flexible, not frozen, Porter's habit was resilience. Rated by adaptability, Porter surely stands at or near the top of any list of Civil War generals. He lived the classic Zen saying, "Six times fall, seven times get up," the image of the leader you would want in charge of your group. One typical morning, with a great battle imminent, Porter sat calmly listening to the click of telegraph keys, patiently alert for information, discussing options under conditions that would have brought others to pace and smoke or drink and swear. Kelly mirrored Porter's eternal calmness, a calmness he presented whether in the face of danger, in reaction to disgrace, or in response to the best of good news. A family member who was with him when he received news of his exoneration said that he showed no emotion. One of his daughters said that she never heard her father laugh.

Porter went through life putting one serious foot in front of the other and it confused people. To this day, in Kelly's images, whether on horseback at the head of his corps in 1862, falling wounded in battle in Mexico, up in the air in a balloon, or at Malvern Hill, Porter appears not terrified or tense but relaxed and self-contained. His unsmiling, tearless tendencies led to misunderstandings. He looked like a statue when others expected something else. Porter's eventual accuser, General Pope, misinterpreted Porter at their first meeting. He could not believe the calm, cool soldier he saw in front of him. Pope wrote that Porter "seemed to exhibit a listlessness and indifference not quite natural under the circumstances, not unusual for men to assume in the midst of dangers and difficulties merely to impress one with their superior coolness." One of Pope's staffers, an excitable colonel named Thomas C.H. Smith, misinterpreted Porter when they met during the unfolding disaster of Second Bull Run. Smith became a major witness against Porter. He testified that he knew on August 29 from Porter's casual deportment and blunt and candid remarks that Porter would fail Pope that day.

It is time to admit bluntly and candidly that Porter's monument failed. The statue was accurate but too ambiguous. People saw the stiff and not the serene, the frozen and not the flexible, the stone wall and not the man. Because Kelly's implications were too subtle, people misinterpreted the statue.

Porter's youngest daughter, Evelina Porter Doggett, spoke angrily about the monument as a distortion of her father's memory. She raised her voice, the nearest to Porter's own that was ever recorded, at an interview in about 1949 with amateur historian Otto Eisenschiml. Eisenschiml, the chemist who invented see-through envelopes, was an avid researcher into mysteries of history. He had made himself controversial in the 1930s when he popularized a conspiracy theory of the assassination of President Lincoln. An indefatigable investigator who specialized in exhaustively-researched Civil War tomes, Eisenschiml also wrote a book about Porter's court-martial and exoneration. Now long out of print, its chief gem is an extended interview with Doggett, then in her eighties, who lived in the General's old homestead in Montclair, New Jersey. When she was asked about the monument, Doggett confronted her interviewer.

"Was my father just a military hero?" she asked.

In her eyes, the monument had failed its purpose.

Eisenschiml noted her reaction with surprise as she rose from her chair to pepper him with more questions—which, like Porter's monument, were fraught with implications.

"Could the statue not have expressed something deeper, something which carries a greater moral than victories in battle? Shall the world, as indicated by Kelly's statue, remember nothing of General Fitz John Porter but his military feats?"

General Porter's passionate spokeswoman, his daughter, was both right and wrong.

Doggett was certainly right that her father was primarily a moral hero rather than a military hero. But her belief that the monument ought to have expressed something deeper, something that carried a greater moral lesson, was wrong because Porter's monument can be decoded and its hidden meaning, Porter's secret, the very secret to which his daughter was obviously privy, can be recovered.

When Kelly created the towering monument, he made Second Bull Run—a pivotal battle of the war, Lee's greatest victory and the Union

Army's most humiliating defeat—invisible. The only Civil War battlefield featured on Porter's monument is Malvern Hill.

The question is, then: why Malvern Hill?

Certainly, not because, at Malvern Hill, Porter's hundred guns shot General Robert E. Lee's finest, bravest, most obedient troops to pieces, mowing them down in rows like a scythe cutting grass. Porter mourned those dead all of his life. He called them his "fellow countrymen." What was significant about Malvern Hill is that it was the battle during which Lee crossed a line that Porter had always held, a line observed by other generals up to that point in Virginia. Confederate General D.H. Hill, who saw the waves of charging troops that Lee sent to their deaths, lamented, "It was not war but murder." Malvern Hill represents Porter's critical state of mind at Second Bull Run. The monument says without words that Porter did not want to follow after General Robert E. Lee.

Accordingly, because the war images on the Porter monument stop with Malvern Hill, and because Second Bull Run is not named, Porter's secret rises between Malvern Hill exactly as it was fought and Second Bull Run as it might have been. Porter's secret is that, at Second Bull Run on August 29, when the tables turned and it was the Union army that would have been mowed down if Porter had ordered his ten-thousand men forward, Porter disobeyed. Porter refused to follow Lee. Porter wrote later of the suicidal charge "as if in reckless disregard of life" that he had witnessed at Malvern Hill. Porter criticized the Union generals who wasted lives in a war of attrition. He wrote about their committing mass murder. As Kelly assembled it, Porter's monument implies that Porter did not follow Pope's order—or Lee's example—on August 29 because of Malvern Hill. His front panel would have been something like "Porter's Last Stand" if he had obeyed General Pope's order and charged on August 29. That front panel is missing. Instead, there are words arranged in the shape of a funeral urn.

As on the Porter monument, so in *Century* magazine.

Porter wrote for *Century* about the nightmare that was Malvern Hill, the battle in which Lee charged Porter's defenses and lost 10,000 men in a couple of hours on July 1, 1862. Porter's account of casualties after the battle form a lugubrious critique. That night he walked the battlefield, where he recalled with pity that he found it hard to put his foot down without stepping on a body.

Or body parts.

Men had been blown apart in the single battle of the war at which most of the casualties were caused by artillery. Many remains could not be identified. The list of Confederate soldiers reported "Missing" skyrocketed at Malvern Hill. *Porter never gloried in gore.* True, Porter's monument was unveiled on the anniversary of Malvern Hill—but that was not Porter's idea. Porter's cousin, Robert H. Eddy, whose bequest funded the monument, required by his will that the monument be unveiled on that day. In short, Cousin Robert wanted to *celebrate* this battle. He was at cross purposes with Porter, who designed a monument to perpetuate the man who learned and humbly followed the moral lesson of Malvern Hill.

Porter never delivered the article on Second Bull Run that he had promised *Century* magazine. Malvern Hill suggests the reason he refused. Porter made Kelly his truth-teller by proxy. On August 29, 1862, when he refused to send his men to death, dismemberment and maiming at the hands of twice their number of Confederate troops under General Longstreet, Porter was refusing to do as Lee had done at Malvern Hill.

The monument failed to communicate the message intended. The public took the monument on its face to depict a military and not a moral hero. On July 1, 1904, for the veterans of the Civil War, civilians and crowds of schoolchildren who stood milling around the monument on the day of its unveiling, Porter had been the brave Union commander at Malvern Hill. While perhaps they ought to have wondered why Bull Run was not named, the omission seems not to have given anyone any pause.

But the figure on horseback alongside the messages on four sides of the Porter monument have always approached and hinted at Porter's moment of greatest moral glory. Porter only once said out loud that he failed Pope and never wrote that he disobeyed Pope's order. He wrote a basketful of different and conflicting reasons for his inaction on August 29: that the order was unclear, that he had discretion, that the order arrived too late in the day to execute, that his staff at the point of the order's receipt persuaded him that the enemy greatly outnumbered the Fifth Corps. But Porter finally let Kelly speak what was in his heart on August 29. The day that Porter made his moral mark in American history between the lines also hovers between the lines on his monument. Porter maintained publicly that he had done everything he could to obey General Pope's suicidal order but he wrote to his wife immediately after his court-martial the much more modest words, "I did nothing of which I need be ashamed."

The gravestone under which Fitz John Porter (1822-1901) and Harriet Pierson Porter (1835-1924) lie buried says as much. After Porter's name and military titles are the words, "He fought the good fight." Carved in stone over his head, they perpetually proclaim Porter to have been a moral man. Arriving at his final resting place, Porter did not give it a rest. He intended that visitors to his grave feel a sense of moral example even if they were unaware of his role at Second Bull Run. The fact that the five words derive from the New Testament, 1 Timothy 6:12 does not change anything. As in Haven Park in Portsmouth, so at the Greenwood Cemetery in Brooklyn, Porter planned how he wanted the country to remember him. Second Bull Run was the "good fight" that was his proudest boast, a boast that prevails even over the silence that normally attends graves.

2

The Hero in His Youth

In his late sixties, Fitz John Porter started an autobiography that he never finished. In it, after saying that his father, Captain John Porter, was once assigned to the Navy Yard in Portsmouth, he offered both of his memories of the city. They were of

— being startled by a snake;
— being pulled up from drowning in some unknown body of water.

Born into a dysfunctional home, Porter seems lucky to have survived. The lessons that he learned in Portsmouth were basically that the world is a dangerous place, that all is not what it appears, that there are snakes in the grass, that one may fall into the water, that an affectionate father may turn into a wild man, and that a mother may not always be able to hold things together.

Porter charily and warily wrote of being born in Portsmouth because his father "so far as I can make out from the scanty records left of him, was stationed there at the time." Captain John's wife, Fitz John's mother, Eliza, wrote cryptically the year after Fitz John's birth, "The life of a public officer is beset with more pains and penalties than the highest renown can ever atone for." On November 11, 1826, shortly before Fitz John, along with his family, left his birthplace at age five, Commodore David Porter raised the subject of his brother John in a letter to his sister, Evalina, only to dismiss it. "I note what you say respecting my unfortunate brother and his family," he said. "It is a cause of great regret to me that he does not mend his ways, but what can I do?"

Porter's monument, the horse's tail-end pointing toward the Navy Yard, stands a few yards from his birthplace and childhood home, thus turning Haven Park into a site where the son's glory overcomes his father's disgrace. Poised and distinguished, the general rides his horse sedately across the street from the house where he spent what seems to have been a miserable childhood. It is as if a statue of Princess Cinderella were set up in a park just across the street from the house where she grew up. The monument in Haven Park celebrates the contrast between Porter's chaotic and helpless early years and his role as the able commander of the Fifth Corps, arguably the best and bravest corps of General George B. McClellan's Army of the Potomac.

Porter's cousin, the attorney who funded the monument, probably very well knew that Porter's childhood haunts were not his favorite place on earth. Avoiding snakes and troubled waters, Cousin Robert suggested in his will Market Square or "some other conspicuous place." It was public opposition to yielding prime public land for a monument to the still-controversial Porter that pushed it into Haven Park. Haven Park, although not an especially conspicuous place, was at least near the historical Porter birthplace. Portsmouth's city fathers neatly stifled most critical voices and satisfied the law concerning wills—snakes and troubled waters be damned.

Baby Fitz's father headed the lesser branch of the "Fighting Porters," America's famous naval family. Captain John Porter was the ne'er-do-well of two brothers who followed famous forbears and joined the Navy. David Long, the biographer of his older brother, Commodore David Porter, wrote incidentally of John, "Evidently, he was often drunk and, when in that condition, he acted with rash bravado. En route to the West Indies, the *Greyhound* ran into a savage storm, and John, well in his cups, refused to shorten sail. His young ensign, later Admiral David Farragut, had to wait for him to disappear below before he could make the necessary adjustment to the rigging and thus save the ship."

Captain John drifted relentlessly toward catastrophe. After the *Greyhound* came the *Boxer*, lost off Belize, British Honduras. According to evidence sleuth Otto Eisenschiml, writing about Captain John's last ship, "although the crew was saved, he had to face a Board of Inquiry." After the Inquiry, Eisenschiml said, Captain John was grounded, "somehow managed to get promoted to Master Commandant, but soon resigned, probably under duress."

Despite Eisenschiml, who echoed wording on the Porter monument's front tablet, it is uncertain that Captain John ever was Commandant of the Naval Yard. Clearly, Porter had no memory of his father as a resplendent Master Commandant whom everybody saluted. Certainly barred from commanding a ship, certainly disabled by alcoholism, Captain John was assigned to land duties *of some type* at the Portsmouth Navy Yard, a job that he, in any case, left or abandoned in the late 1820s.

Captain John's last port of call was, ironically, Watertown, Massachusetts. One wonders if he labored at the Watertown Arsenal, or if he even worked at all. The father that Fitz John remembered would have been a moody, chronically ill man in impoverished disgrace who died in October, 1831, shortly after Fitz John turned nine. Fitz John wrote not a word about his father's death. Transparently, his memories of Watertown were not even as nostalgic as the two he had of Portsmouth. Without anything or anybody to keep her in Massachusetts, Captain John's widow, Eliza, shook free of any "Fighting Porter" mystique and promptly headed as far away as she could get with her four children, three boys and a baby girl. She set up or ran a private school for girls in Alexandria, Virginia.

In Alexandria, Eliza enrolled Fitz John in a local boys' school, where he seems to have been bullied. At Benjamin Hallowell's school, Fitz John confronted a pecking order between "uptown" and "downtown" boys that disfavored a poor working widow's son. Having grown up in chaos far worse than any bullying boys' school, Fitz John might have bounced back. However, his mother instead decided that Alexandria was no fit place for him. She sent him north to Phillips Academy in Exeter, New Hampshire. Then, when that did not work, Fitz John was consigned to a schoolmaster who taught out of his home in Jamaica Plain, Massachusetts, on the outskirts of Boston. In that teacher's home, Porter at last stayed in a school long enough to thrive. The schoolmaster, Stephen M. Weld, became Fitz John's surrogate father, mentor and lifelong friend.

If one's childhood experiences are important, if our characters are shaped by the first several years of our lives, then it was in Portsmouth, Watertown, Alexandria, Exeter, and Boston that Fitz John Porter first worked out his strategy for dealing with life. Given an alcoholic father who was unreliable and a mother who, at least eventually, had little time or patience for him, Fitz John discovered and cultivated a high degree of self-reliance and resilience. Schoolmaster Weld most likely welcomed into his family a wary and reserved boy ever alert to danger but determined to manage anyway. A boy who had never experienced a loving, functioning family, with Weld, was in another world, a suddenly safer one. The adaptable lad soon bonded with his hospitable teacher, blended into the Weld family and was later recalled by one of its members contentedly, his thoughts his own, taking his turn rocking the latest Weld baby to sleep. Between overseeing Fitz John's integration into his family and teaching other students, Weld seems to have made a very successful effort to boost Fitz John's confidence and his mathematical and verbal proficiency. After a couple of cradle-rocking and intensive years of study in Jamaica Plain, the young man was ready to take his examination for West Point.

Nothing survives from which to reconstruct why Fitz John went into the Army. In Porter's youth, the Army was a ticket west when young Americans were going west rather than to sea. Eisenschiml wrote awkwardly, without explanation or source, that "the sole ambition of his mother, who knew the deceptive glamour of armed service so well, was to secure for him admittance to West Point." Porter had discussed with Kelly a *bas relief* of his parents' joint portrait, hardly to honor the major influence of his father on his life. Perhaps his poor mother *did* think well of West Point and its free education. If so, with his mother's blessing, Fitz John's wise teacher-father surrogate might have encouraged him to join a branch of service where he could make his own name without either having to live down his father's reputation or having to live up to records set by successful Porters. Perhaps Fitz John joined the Army *because* all of the other Porters joined the Navy! The mystery remains intriguing but unanswerable. Especially as the parental portrait idea was tossed, Porter's monument does not touch upon the answer even by implication.

Weld prepared Porter well. The Phillips Academy drop-out from a dysfunctional family, tutored in Boston, passed the United States Military Academy examinations. Fitz John's small boarding school exerted its last small pull on him. Porter was a cadet in the classes on which "the stars fell," classes that would provide the officers in the highest ranks during the Civil War. Forever grateful, early in the war, General Porter took his teacher's son under wing as a second aide on his personal staff. The hardships of army life were thus mitigated for Stephen M. Weld, Jr., who, as the General's aide, had his own orderly to chop wood, fetch water and set up and stock a tent in which, insulated from the damp and cold by a wooden platform, Weld wrote back happily to his father in Boston.

General Porter returned the favor of surrogate fatherhood, little imagining that he was headed for a court-martial at which Weld would be one of several sympathetic but unavailing witnesses preceding President Lincoln's approval of an order that he forfeit his rank and be barred from holding any Federal office forever.

3

The Wounded Warrior:
Porter Before the Belén Gate

Around the statue's oversized granite pedestal, besides the front tablet are three war scenes in *bas relief*. In order of chronology, the first one displays young Lieutenant Porter on the ground, wounded during the Mexican War on September 13, 1847.

One of the star cadets at West Point, ranking eighth out of a class of forty-one upon his graduation in 1845, Porter soon found himself fighting a war south of the border. Ulysses S. Grant, later General Grant, wrote in his memoirs that the Mexican War was unjustified, an "unholy" aggression spurred on by slave-holders lusting for territory to be made into new slave states. Unlike Grant, another participant, Edward Mansfield, crowed exuberantly as a nation-builder in his popular 1849 pot-boiler *The Mexican War* that "the Mexicans uniformly, in their reports and letters, speak of the people of the United States of the north, as 'Americans,' although they are themselves just as much 'Americans.' This settles the question, whether the people of the United States have a *name*."

Porter's first assignment was to Fort Polk, the Army's reinforcement depot at Point Isabel, Texas. There, in an exotic but deadly setting, Porter wrote Robert Henry Eddy, his slightly older cousin, the man who would later fund the Porter monument. In his letter dated on his birthday, August 31, 1846, Porter told Eddy how he pitied the many soldiers added to the heaps of graves now rising a half mile from here. Poor sufferers, they knew not the trials & troubles of a volunteer's life. Bivouacking in the open air with no tents to shield from the sun for their aching bones, or shelter them from the pouring rains is not what they anticipated when they rushed with so much patriotism to arms. Judging from the remarks of most of their officers, I fancy the pleasures of home would be far more satisfactory to them, than all the honors they hope to reap.

Porter also told his cousin that he was "shamefully disappointed" to be "out of the reach of danger and honor."

That changed.

Soon enough, howitzers were needed and the West Point-trained artillerist took part in the siege of Vera Cruz, and battles at Cerro Gordo and Contreras, on the way to the hardest nut to crack, Mexico City.

Like most Civil War generals, including Grant and Lee, Porter was a Mexican War veteran. On the monument, with Porter's guidance, Kelly depicted him knocked out of the saddle by a spent cannonball. The tablet says, in effect, "I was wounded. I was nearly killed. When I was young, I saw others die in battle." (Photo courtesy of Doug Kerr)

Approaching Mexico City, Porter was within reach of danger and of honor. High above Mexico City in a castle complex fortified by light and heavy artillery, a fortress, Chapultepec's defenders could fire down and throw a hail of shells over any attackers. General Winfield Scott plotted a three-step plan to take Mexico City. First, the Americans, regulars and volunteers, were to take El Molino del Rey ("The King's Mill"), a stone-walled cannon foundry and powder mill at the foot of Chapultepec; second, they were to attack uphill against a rain of bullets and artillery shells and capture Chapultepec; and, third, they would come down, wheel and storm the two gates of San Cosme and Belén. In the opinion of Grant, who stormed San Cosme, the three-step plan was too many steps by two. Grant wrote, "In later years, if not at the time, the battles of Molino del Rey and Chapultepec have seemed to me wholly unnecessary. When the assaults upon the garitas of San Cosme and Belén were determined upon, the road running east to the former gate could have been reached easily, without an engagement while, in like manner, the troops designated to act against Belén could have kept east of Chapultepec, out of range." Improbably, Scott's complicated and dangerous three-step plan worked, although it also generated the war's highest casualties. Eventually among the wounded himself, Porter took part in all three phases of the battle for Mexico City.

The first phase was conducted blindly. There was no intelligence, in either the technical or the ordinary meaning of that word. Nobody knew what the Americans faced. As a military action, El Molino del Rey turned out to be a charge by forces who were outnumbered three or four to one. Serving under his doomed Captain Simon H. Drum and buoyed up by intrepid enthusiasts alongside of him, Porter stormed Molina del Rey, the site that supposedly had to fall first, and then Chapultepec. Porter was commended for artillery support of infantry while "continually exposing himself during the action to a heavy fire."

At last at the Belén Gate, Porter was more than exposed; he was hit. Porter was "knocked down by a spent cannon ball which struck his shoulder," according to his friend and would-be biographer, the San Francisco attorney Theodore Lord, who would have learned the details from Porter himself.

Six times fall, seven times get up.

Resilience, Porter's most consistent trait!

A few dazed minutes after he went down, Porter rose up to rejoin Captain Drum.

He was boosted by a swig of brandy on the way. He told the story during a June, 1900 conversation between himself and General O.O. Howard, of which Kelly made notes that Styple published:

> Howard: General Porter was telling me that in the Mexican War, some officers had a foreboding about their death and several of them were killed in that battle for Mexico City.
>
> Porter: Yes, there was a general feeling of gloom and apprehension that morning.
>
> I remember one officer, he was sitting on the base of a column of the aqueduct moaning and I said, "Cheer up" and offered him my flask of brandy which revived him.
>
> Howard: The officer was moaning, referring to his hurt—
>
> Porter: No, the bullet had struck his eyeglasses and merely bruised him—a little later he came along the same road and found me in the same position—I was doubled up—so he handed the flask to me and said, "Now let me do for you what you did for me."

Aided by passing infantry, Porter ran the unit's howitzer up to the front, where he loaded and fired, peppering the enemy with canister shot until ammunition ran low. Captain Drum sent his "walking wounded" lieutenant to ride back for an ammunition cart. Porter, under fire, returned only to find Captain Drum and the other senior officer dead. Mid-battle, Porter was suddenly in command—with "little left to command." Of the enlisted men of the Fourth Artillery only three of an original twenty-seven men were alive and unhurt.

Another officer who observed the battered Porter at that time never forgot what he saw. Porter, one of few men left standing, braved heavy fire to load, aim and fire his howitzer almost single-handedly until the gate was breached. Some twenty years later and far from Mexico, William Loring—by then General Loring—had never seen a braver act by any man than Porter's at the Belén Gate. As reported during the well-publicized world tour that Grant took after his Presidency:

General Grant, while visiting Egypt during his trip around
the world, met General William W. Loring, who occupied
the position of Inspector General of the Khedive's Army.

At the storming of Mexico City Loring had commanded the regiment of infantry to which Porter's battery
had been attached, and in the course of the conversation
Grant said, "Loring, I suppose you have seen as much
fighting as anybody. What was the bravest act you ever
saw on any battlefield?"

Without hesitation Loring answered, "Fitz John
Porter at the assault on the City of Mexico."

Porter's actions were officially recorded and rewarded. General
Scott awarded Porter a brevét promotion to Major "for gallant and conspicuous conduct." Nonetheless, on Kelly's panel of Belén Gate, the artist's focus is not upon bravery in action but upon a wounded man going
down. An old soldier, his arms up in dismay, rushes to help the fallen
Porter. The bearded veteran, standing under fire, his back a fine target
for snipers, is not realistic. He is Kelly's invention, a device to direct a
viewer's eyes to the fallen figure of Porter on the ground. The tablet says,
in effect, "I was wounded. I was nearly killed. When I was young, I saw
others die in battle."

As briefly summarized on the front panel of his monument,
Porter the war veteran made the Army his career. He was soon reas-
signed to West Point as a Cavalry and Artillery instructor. New Superintendent Robert E. Lee made him his adjutant. A good soldier who did
well enough but did not seem to like teaching, Porter bonded with his
fellow instructors, including George B. McClellan, who became a close
friend. Because Porter, the widow's son, was careful with his pennies,
he was a target touched by his less frugal friends on occasion for loans.
Quite approachable by his peers, Porter was considered an iceberg by
his students. A biographer who requested recollections of Porter from his
cadets received few replies. Except for one who vividly recalled Porter
in a pinch, when he efficiently took charge of cadets to avoid dropping
a piece of heavy ordnance that nearly slipped and could have crushed
them, and another cadet instructed in artillery by Porter who confessed
"a boy's admiration for his gallant bearing, his *sang froid*, and his soldierly knowledge," surviving cadets wrote back frank recollections of a

man who was "dignified—not easy to approach or be familiar with—cold, haughty perhaps" and "a proud man—perhaps haughty." He was obviously not running Weld's school at West Point.

Porter was assigned in 1856 to "Bleeding Kansas." After that, he took part in General Johnson's mission to bring order to Mormon country in Utah. Porter exulted in dealing with what he thought were important problems. Exotic landscapes aside, Porter the nation-builder was intent on bringing law and order to parts of the country terrorized by what he

Porter was the Army officer who developed the idea of shifting the Union force in Charleston from its vulnerable battery on shore to the unfinished fort in the middle of Charleston Harbor, Fort Sumter. He went South incognito to make arrangements for this successfully secret move. Porter's choice shaped a war that began with first shots exploding over Fort Sumter. (Photo courtesy of the Library of Congress; James Erik, http://JamesErik.com.)

viewed as zealots or religious fanatics. Porter made no attempt to charm or to persuade. "The point of a gun was the only law" he thought would be understood. Whether because of the Army or in spite of the Army, the cascade of lawlessness and violence in Kansas and then in Utah was reduced to a trickle.

Porter engaged literally in some activities outside the Army. In the spring of 1857, the iceberg melted. Porter, almost 35 years old, was ready for marriage. His bride was the 21-year-old Harriet Pierson, of an old New York family. They went on to have four children and seemed to be devoted to one another and to their children although, unlike some memoirists, Porter never brought up his family in his writings. As a gentleman of Victorian sensibilities, Porter seems to have determined that one's family was a private matter to which one tastefully made no public reference.

Porter was pulled into Washington by the head of the Army, his old Mexican War chief, General Winfield Scott, when Lincoln was elected in November 1860 and war looked imminent. Together, Scott and Porter hastily identified hot spots where Federal installations made trouble most likely, including Charleston, South Carolina, and coastal Texas. Independent of President Buchanan and his Secretary of War, they decided that aging Colonel Gardner had to be replaced in Charleston, South Carolina. According to William Bender Wilson, a War Department telegraph operator who published his memoirs in 1892, Porter made a secret trip to Charleston, where he identified Major Robert Anderson as the one Scott should make the Union commandant. Evidence corroborates Wilson. Porter initialed his annotation to the last page of his November 11, 1860 "Inspection Report of Forts Moultrie & Sumpter and Castle Pinkney in Charleston Harbor," now at the New York Historical Society, "I argued successfully the assignment of Major Robert Anderson. He was the proper person to send there, being of the regiment, without exciting suspicion of intention to reinforce the garrison—Moreover, he was an experienced & able officer, of unblemished integrity and true to his Government whose commission he held."

Wilson claimed further that "Anderson's plan to evacuate Fort Moultrie was worked out in a conference between General Winfield Scott and Porter, but that this arrangement, at Scott's request, was kept secret from the Buchanan Administration." Thus, defensible Fort Sumter in Charleston harbor was to be occupied. One dark December night, to the complete surprise not only of the Confederates and also of the Buchanan Administration, Major Anderson evacuated the on-shore vulnerable Fort Moultrie. Porter's pivotal role behind Fort Sumter was a secret until long after the war.

Next, still without President Buchanan's knowledge, Porter sped arms and ammunition on their way in quantity to Union-loyal civilians to defend Missouri from falling into Confederate hands. Then, the Navy brought Porter to a place familiar to him from the Mexican War: He initiated and oversaw the sudden evacuation of all soldiers and government property from Texas.

No fame arose from these secret missions. Proud of his 1861 services, services that he always thought raised him above others during that period, Porter showed sculptor Kelly books that referred to his work organizing troops in Pennsylvania early in 1861. He wryly told Kelly, "I have sent copies to Portsmouth as I do not want them to think that I am asking space for a statue to some obscure individual."

During the week of Fort Sumter, Porter wrote an urgent letter to his old comrade, George B. McClellan, asking that he rejoin the army. McClellan called Porter's invitation welcome. Because "Little Mac" was quickly snapped up by Ohio to lead its volunteers, it was a while before he rejoined the regular Army. McClellan was, thus, visible when a vacancy arose for President Lincoln to fill. Wanting

Both veterans of the Mexican War, Porter and McClellan seemed to have first met after the war when they were both instructors at West Point. Friends then, friends forever, the week that Fort Sumter fell, Porter wrote then-civilian McClellan to leave off running a railroad and to rejoin the Army. After he did and President Lincoln appointed "Little Mac" to head the Army of the Potomac, Mac appointed Porter to head one of his Army's six corps. (Photo courtesy of the Library of Congress; James Erik, http://JamesErik.com.)

to replace General Irvin McDowell as head of the Army of the Potomac after the Union disaster of First Bull Run in June, 1861, Lincoln asked McClellan; and, when McClellan agreed, McClellan in turn asked Porter to become one of his six corps commanders. McDowell, McClellan and Porter were then and thereafter fatefully connected. McClellan fell out of favor in the last half of 1862. Accused of having caused the Union disaster at Second Bull Run, the "McClellanist" Porter was thrown out of the Army. McDowell, whom Porter eventually and reluctantly identified as cause of the catastrophe at Second Bull Run, stayed in the Army, lived long and collected his general's pension, retiring to San Francisco in 1882. McDowell is buried at the Presidio. Porter is buried in Brooklyn. The chief difference in their afterlives is that Porter has a monument.

4

The Aerial Spy:
Porter over Yorktown

I n the spring of 1862 General Porter escaped the war by balloon. Unafraid of flying, he enjoyed frequent holidays of peace and quiet high above everything while, officially, he served as McClellan's eye in the sky on the rebels.

Porter was a fearless flyer. He took to the air like a bird, ascending over a hundred times over the armies of the Blue and Grey. According to Professor Thaddeus S.C. Lowe, the expert in ballooning, Porter was uniquely enthusiastic among all of the Union officers, including "Boy General" Custer, who turned white and shook. (Photo courtesy of Doug Kerr)

Porter's enthusiasm for flight was unique. Among the Union high command, no one else ascended so often or with such serene pleasure. Professor Thaddeus S.C. Lowe, America's most famous balloonist or "aeronaut," ran the fledgling air-spy service during the Civil War. Professor Lowe was in the ideal position to compare Union commanders whom he personally took up hundreds of feet in the air, higher than Confederate rifles or cannon could reach. According to Professor Lowe, the Commander of the Army of the Potomac, General McClellan, went up once but "trembled and changed color." The "Boy General," George Armstrong Custer, later famous for "Custer's Last Stand," lost enthusiasm by the yard until he was "physically white and shivering like an aspen leaf." Only Porter, who made at least a hundred balloon ascents to an altitude of at least 1,000 feet in order to be well above the 300-foot range of guns, was "perfectly cool and brave…always."

Ironically, soldiers on the ground who saw an officer in uniform distant and high above them thought that McClellan was overhead watching them. Private Thomas Mann, a soldier with the 18th Massachusetts Regiment, wrote home that he saw that "McClellan made his daily trips into the air by means of a large balloon, under the charge of Prof. Lowe." Moreover, Mann commended not Porter but Little Mac as "the first general commanding an army to use the balloon for military purposes."

Nothing could reduce Porter's appetite for sky work. After April 11, 1862, when he survived the scariest flight of his life, he turned his near-disaster into a funny story. "The General could have fallen to his death" became a comic tale suitable for children. As his best and only known imitation of a humorist, Porter took pleasure in recounting his runaway ride.

"This was one of the few tales of the past which we were often told when we were children," his daughter confirmed to Otto Eisenschiml.

At some point, probably well after the war, Porter wrote up his comic story. Porter's daughter gave the Library of Congress the unpublished manuscript, which bears the misleadingly sober title "Signal and Balloon Services." It is boxed along with a fantastic artifact, a carefully-drawn, pen-and-ink sketch of Confederate defenses that Porter made in the air, the first fruit of American aerial reconnaissance.

1

Signal and
— The Balloon Services —

Early in our troubles in 1861 the Uses of the Balloon and Signal Service organizations became a subject of attentive interest to many officers and of great and increasing value.

The Signal Service had for a few years been a part of the army organization, but its application by instruction had been mainly limited to New Mexico, though several officers of noted intelligence had become familiar with the system then under the care of Maj Myers an assistant Surgeon of the army a gentleman from civil life who was devoted to its useful application and extension.

Against its extended application a strong prejudice prevailed and had become somewhat fixed from the fact that some of the best instructed officers, who had gone to the Southern army, were familiar with the system and would be able to read our messages — which would thus be as useful to foes as to friends — an objection which had no greater force than objections to the use of different cyphers on telegraph lines.

Knowing the uses of the system and that it would be of great value to have signal communication between the forces about Washington and General Patterson's army near Harper's Ferry, especially when the former should advance on Manassas, I, then chief of Staff to Gen Patterson, tried to have communication established, but probably because of ignorance of its importance joined to the fact of there being but few well instructed & trusted employees, very little attention was given to the matter at Washington and the effort failed.

Communication was attempted to be maintained by telegraph through Baltimore, but the despatches were so delayed as to be useless sometimes on receipt — because inapplicable to the situation.

Porter published his memoir of the Battles of Gaines's Mills and Malvern Hill, but never published his memoir of his days high in the air over everything. He was an enthusiastic and imperturbably tranquil "aeronaut," or balloonist. (Photo courtesy of the Library of Congress; James Erik, http://JamesErik.com.)

Porter in the air was an excited, exhilarated, productive and joyful man.

"I undertook to use what little influence I possessed in having the balloon party brought within my command," Porter recalled. "Safely suspended in the air some hundreds of feet I often watched, with a good field glass, the country in front of our army and became familiar with the country and the roads."

But Porter was not safely suspended on April 11, 1862. Nor had he felt well that morning. Quite sick, Porter would have stayed on the ground; but somebody, presumably McClellan himself, wanted an updated report on the enemy's defenses and had ordered a survey from the air. Porter said, sanely enough, that he "would have resisted compliance had there been anyone available who was accustomed to the service or had the information not been so essential to future operations."

Three weeks after Porter's "runaway balloon" flight, Yorktown fell. Yorktown was an empty victory, however. McClellan captured a village and farms of no strategic value that were simply abandoned by the Confederates, who chose their departure time after they had delayed "Little Mac's" advance upon Richmond while they fortified that city. (Photo courtesy of the Library of Congress; James Erik, http://JamesErik.com.)

Ironically, even the balloon scene, the first of the Porter monument Civil War panels, was shadowed by Porter's consideration of resistance to complying with an order, although on that date he reasoned out an affirmative answer.

His compliance nearly killed him.

That morning just before sunrise, when Porter was in his seat in the basket, still alone on the aircraft, awaiting Professor Lowe, his military balloon broke free from its mooring. Normally fastened to a groundwork by two ropes, the balloon began to rise unexpectedly when only one rope was secured. A few rods up, that single tether snapped and the balloon instantly took off, flying upward at what Porter called "a fearful rate."

"Looking down over the basket—always dreaded and avoided if possible as dizzying—I saw my helplessness," Porter said. Tongue-in-cheek, he added that he "could not swap vehicles or jump out."

But he could cry out and he did, yelling, "What shall I do?"

"Pull on the valve!" someone below shouted back up.

Porter looked up and saw not one but two cords dangling. This part of balloon operations was always the professor's job while Porter kept his eyes on the Confederates.

When Porter found that he could not jump quite high enough to reach them, he seized on the idea of climbing the ropes. Anyone reading his manuscript can hear the father telling the exciting story to his children:

"Climb I did and placing the cords between my teeth descended sufficiently I thought to be in the basket when, kicking out, I failed to find it and feared the basket had drifted from under me. Horrors!"

Looking down, Porter aimed to drop in the basket, dropped accurately, then sat, noting that "the perspiration rolled from me." He fastened the cord and pulled on the valve, lowering the balloon. As he smelled escaping gas, rather than worrying, he was exhilarated. Valve in hand, a sensation of omnipotence possessed him. He wrote about this intoxicating part of his memory at length:

"I held the reins. My alarm instantly vanished. To this day the varying and intoxicating scenes and some important events are impressed in my mind and as clear and fresh as if the events were now before me; wagons looked little larger than ants, men were only discernible when in groups. Still the sound of voices was very distinct as if reflected from a sounding board above. I observed the defenses around Yorktown, the camps and field works of the enemy along the line of the Warwick River.

Richmond was in plain view, as also Fort Monroe and Norfolk—the waters from which were enlivened by a small steamer coming down the James River—the appearance of the *Merrimack* on the Elizabeth River and of the *Monitor* in Hampton Roads, all moving."

But on April 11 the *Monitor* and *Merrimack*, having famously fought to a draw in early March, were only posturing. They would never meet again. The rebels would scuttle and burn the *Merrimack* in May to prevent its capture. Porter, drifting over Yorktown, paid no further attention to the cutting edges of modern naval warfare and experimented only with aeronautics. Turned pilot, the practical Porter located ephemeral currents and cross-currents that he could take back toward the Union camp. At his single control, he shifted his altitude to catch the right winds. All the giddy time, he said, he took mental notes on rebel defenses. Orders were orders.

Porter's control of the balloon disappeared as he neared the ground and the balloon both sped up and literally ran out of gas,

General Porter with his feet on the ground, with staff. He discussed his runaway flight with staff as if it had been a joy ride of no consequence, emphasizing that he was unhurt and "had hurt nobody else" in crash landing on a tent. Porter is standing figure on far right. (Photo courtesy of the Library of Congress; James Erik, http://JamesErik.com.)

suddenly dropping "like a lump of lead" over the edge of the Union Army's camp. Porter might have become the first American pilot to die in a crash except that the basket hit the ridge pole of a wall tent, which saved him. Tumbling down from the tent, the agile General found his footing before he was mobbed by Baxter's Zouaves. They mistook him for Professor Lowe, a misidentification Porter did not care to correct. Instead, the "professor" quickly drew himself up and asked to be taken to their leader. Dropping in next on a surprised General Burns, a still-exuberant Porter grinned and cheerily quoted Shakespeare, "A horse! A kingdom for a horse!"

As Porter told his children, he galloped on the borrowed horse over to General McClellan's tent, where officers just ordered to organize a search for his body saw him coming and ran to tell McClellan. Forewarned, when Porter arrived, McClellan put his pen down casually and said, "Hello, Fitz! I was wondering who to put in your place."

A surviving McClellan letter corroborates Porter's account. Mac described what he called his "terrible scare" in a letter to his wife. McClellan had first reacted to news of Porter's runaway flight by personally riding to the outer pickets, where he heard a rumor that Porter had touched down three miles away, behind enemy lines. McClellan then returned to headquarters, where he drafted a search order, "but the order had no sooner gone than in walks Mr. Fitz just as cool as usual." Anticipating her worry, McClellan assured his wife that he would not go up in "the confounded balloon."

Lieutenant Weld, the son of Porter's Boston schoolmaster, wrote in his diary that he was in his tent at dawn, not yet dressed, when his orderly ran in and said, "General Porter's balloon has broken loose and he is sailing over us." When Weld rushed out, about a mile up, he saw the speck of a balloon. As he followed it, the speck sailed toward the enemies' tents but gradually came back over the Union camp, until it descended rapidly.

"As General Porter afterwards told me," Weld wrote, "when he found the balloon had broken loose, he looked around for the ropes to pull the valve to let out the gas. He found to his dismay that they were tied six or eight feet up in the netting, away from the car. So all he could do was to climb up, while a mile up in the air, into this netting, get hold of the ropes, climb down into the car again, and then, when a current of wind took him over our camp, open the valves and pull on the ropes.

2 pieces of Artillery (field) keep the enemy engaged and drive their men from their camps.

Ascended in balloon at 6, O'Clock and examined carefully the works around York and along Warwick River. My Sketch is as follows. — Some portions such as the flanks of bastions I could not see — and hence some which appear as lunettes may be bastions. Am convinced of the great strength of the place and that the enemy has made his position

This he did with all his vigor, and he came down, landing on a shelter tent, without being hurt or hurting any one else."

Weld noted that, immediately after his heart-stopping flight, Porter seemed only giddy, "a little overcome by the fumes of the gas, but that was all."

Historically inaccurate as a double exposure, Kelly's panel on the Porter monument morphs two authentic scenes. First, Porter in profile is the man that Mann saw, and that Professor Lowe knew, the ever-calm Porter with binoculars whose constant presence overhead forced the rebels to make their major moves under cover of night or the dense forest outside Yorktown. During Porter's elevated observations, Mann knew and reported the Confederates wasted "several tons of iron trying to reach it with their best rifled guns." Kelly only hinted at the runaway balloon aspect. The sculptor made nothing of Porter's agility and athletic ability as a virtual acrobat. The only sculpted suggestion of Porter's wild and dangerous ride is the balloon's dangling gas vent. Kelly bled the humor and the life out of an adventure that Porter told in comic form with a punch line. What was Kelly after? He wanted to impress in the mind of any visitor an image of Porter as serene, a sane man who could and would keep his head despite any obstacles, to study the landscape and gauge the enemy's strength and intentions. In other words, what he did a thousand feet up, Porter could do and would do with both feet on the ground in the middle of the Second Battle of Bull Run.

LEFT: Up in the air, Porter sketched what he saw below in the way West Point taught its draughtsmen, including topographic icons for defense works. What Porter spied from the balloon he copied carefully into his pocket notebook, to be handy at any moment in the field or in conferences with General McClellan. (Photo courtesy of the Library of Congress; James Erik, http://JamesErik.com.)

5

Lee's Antagonist:
Porter at Gaines's Mill and Malvern Hill

From his monument in Portsmouth, Porter fired his last shot at General Robert E. Lee. Lee took charge of the Army of Northern Virginia when General Joseph E. Johnston was wounded on May 31, 1862. In quick succession, Porter took Lee's best shots in two battles, the first at Gaines's Mill, the second at Malvern Hill, winning each time.

Lee and Porter knew one another personally. Although never very comfortable together, they did share experiences in war and peace. Both men served in the Mexican War. However, Lee was a brevet major and finally colonel who saw the war as one of Scott's staff. Lee probably heard of the brave lieutenant. He may even have seen Porter in heroic action before the Belén Gate, a scene depicted on the monument. Neither Lee nor Porter wrote of meeting during the Mexican War nor of their later, closer work together. During Porter's five years at West Point, when Lee was the Superintendent, Porter was his adjutant.

Lee was busy when Porter, nestled in a comfortable wooden house in the small Virginia hamlet of Beaver Dam, uncharacteristically lyrical, as if there had been no battles recently, observed the "clear and bright" dawn of June 26, 1862. As was his habit, Porter kept his head while others were losing theirs. To him, everything seemed quiet and peaceful. Porter recalled a somnolent morning spent "sitting for hours near the telegraph operator at my quarters, prior to the attack, listening to the constant and rapid 'ticking' of his instrument." News was deciphered and set before him like clockwork. Union scouts checking enemy camps sent dispatches that they were "largely deserted." Only if Porter ventured outside of his cozy niche, where vast clouds of dust rose high over the northern and western horizons throughout that day, did he see evidence that the enemy was on the move and that a storm was brewing.

Officers who had been present when Mexico City fell in 1847 felt certain that a Confederate collapse was imminent. Collapse required only a catalyst and Union victories could supply that catalyst. Grant wrote in his *Memoirs* that "up to the battle of Shiloh I, as well as thousands of other citizens, believed that the rebellion against the Government would collapse suddenly and soon, if a decisive victory could be gained over any of its armies. Forts Donelson and Henry were such victories." From Grant's victories at Forts Henry and Donelson, Porter himself calculated that an overall rebel collapse would come soon. In a February 8, 1862 letter Porter's aide, Lieutenant Weld,

General Robert E. Lee attacked but never defeated Porter at Gaines's Mills and Malvern Hill. Indeed, at Malvern Hill, Lee's casualties were so huge that Porter knew that Lee had left Richmond wide open for an immediate assault. Porter made a midnight ride on July 1 to beg General "Mac" McClellan to attack, but Mac was invested in a retreat from Virginia soil, something he called a "relocation of headquarters." (Photo courtesy of the Library of Congress; James Erik, http://JamesErik.com.)

wrote, "After reading the account of the taking of Fort Henry, General Porter said that now, unless some terrible blunder was made, we were sure of beating them, i.e., rebels, everywhere we met them." Amazingly, Porter foresaw a second battle at Bull Run (or "Manassas," its alternate name) coming that would determine the war. On February 17, 1862 Weld noted Porter's bold prediction that "we should be in Richmond within six weeks, unless the rebels laid down their arms before that time—but he also thinks that the rebels will not give up until they are whipped at Manassas, so you see, I am glad to say, that we stand a fair chance of having a battle before the war is over."

It would be so and Porter, not McClellan, would fight it in August, but in the early summer of 1862 McClellan, creeping cautiously up to the rebel capital, even hearing the bells of Richmond's churches, nearly tasted victory before fearing a trap. Hesitating, he was soon outflanked by J.E.B. Stuart's cavalry. Then, when given a mighty push by Jackson's troops, Mac began to feel his way back. Slowly, very slowly, he edged toward the James River, still wavering between retreating and attacking.

Mac came to consult with Porter at his comfortable headquarters late on June 26. They discussed two options. If Mac retreated, Porter's Fifth Corps would be reinforced where he was, at Beaver Dam: in that case, Porter would stay only to cover the main army's retreat before retreating himself. The other plan was different: under it, Mac would launch a great war-ending assault on Richmond while Porter and his Fifth Corps would be sacrificed to stop Lee from pursuing McClellan. Porter's job would be to rush to Gaines's Mill, to step into Lee's guns' sights, and to re-enact the Alamo.

As recounted in a letter to historian John C. Ropes, Porter said that:

> McClellan left me after 12 o'clock that night to decide, after returning to his headquarters, whether I should remain at Beaver Dam and be reinforced or move as quick as possible to the selected position at Gaines's Mill where I would be reinforced from the right bank, or McClellan would attack Richmond and I resist Lee's attack even to my destruction, thereby to prevent Lee from going to the defense of Richmond.

McClellan's order to Porter the next day was that he move to Gaines's Mill.

Porter recalled, "I felt that the life or death of the army depended upon our conduct in the contest that day, and that on the issue of that contest depended an early peace or a prolonged, devastating war."

Certain that McClellan was on his way south, Porter dug in at Gaines's Mill. The great Civil War historian Stephen Sears summarized the Battle of Gaines's Mill concisely, "The struggle began at noon and lasted almost nine hours and throughout its course it was believed at Porter's headquarters (according to Major Webb of the artillery staff) that they were fighting for time to enable the rest of the army to smash its way into Richmond." Then, late in the day, reinforcements rode up along with unexpected word that McClellan had changed his mind. McClellan was going to retreat.

Porter's reinforcements included some of the most fearless troops in the Union army. Sculptor Kelly must have exulted when Porter first mentioned the Irish Brigade. For Kelly, a city boy during the Draft Riots of 1863 which shamed its predominantly Irish participants, which stigmatized New York's Irish as sympathizers with the enemy, the Irish Brigade, the "Fighting 69th," was the redemption of his people. Colorful General Thomas Francis "Meagher of the Sword" Meagher, who led the Brigade, was an expatriate with a thick brogue who personally recruited toughs like himself off the streets of New York to fight the rebels. Kelly must have known immediately that he wanted Meagher's image and name on Porter's monument. It was justifiable because, at Gaines's Mill, Meagher rode up with his green flag flying just as "fighting engulfed the entire front, with the Confederate units mixing and fighting and dying together." Meagher officially reported that he:

> came upon the hill where the main hospital of the Union army had been established and where a greater portion of our broken and retreating forces were assembled. My brigade reached the summit of this hill in two lines of battle and, having reached it, despite of the cavalry, artillery, and infantry that were breaking through them, preserved an unwavering and undaunted front. Our advance, which was repeatedly assailed by the shells and the round shot of the enemy, did not halt until commanded to do so by General Fitz John Porter, who gave the command in person. At this time the firing of the enemy suddenly ceased on our front and opened on our right, in consequence of which General Porter directed me to move by brigade obliquely to the right and so relieve the regulars occupying the ground which these splendid troops had so gallantly maintained all through the desperate conflict of the day and long after their ammunition had been exhausted.

But Jackson's troops forced Porter back. Lieutenant Weld, who had been captured early that morning and held in a church, "heard the most tremendous firing going on between Stonewall Jackson's forces and ourselves. Prisoners of ours kept coming in during the whole day, and it was not until the end of the day that Jackson was successful." Sent to Richmond and held for six weeks at Libby Prison until he was exchanged in one of the last prisoner exchanges of the war, Weld returned with General John F. Reynolds, the highest-ranking prisoner of war. At Second Bull Run, Reynolds and Weld would have front row seats again.

Porter dropped back to a strong position that was literally carved out of Malvern Hill in three days flat. Hundreds of trees were felled, rough-hewn, and built up into a horseshoe-shaped fortification that hugged and melted back into the thickly-forested hill. Porter, the professor of artillery at West Point, and McClellan's chief of artillery, Colonel Hunt, expertly set a hundred guns, large and small, to cover the valley below with cross-fire. As recognized at the time and by historians ever since, the Union position was virtually impregnable. "As the Federals withdrew, their mass tightened like a fist," Donald Davis put it succinctly in *Stonewall Jackson*. James McPherson said similarly of Porter's position, "one hundred and fifty feet high and flanked by deep ravines a mile apart, Malvern Hill would have to be attacked frontally and uphill across open fields."

With Porter and Hunt, McClellan watched with satisfaction as the breastworks and guns were pushed and hauled into place. Riding back to headquarters, McClellan had no concern about the strength of Malvern Hill. He knew that anyone who attempted to breach Malvern Hill would simply die. Attacking uphill while exposed to both light and heavy artillery—the hundred guns—would be virtually suicidal. McClellan sent word to Washington that he planned to rest his forces. He expected Lee to view the Union array of strength and weaponry at Malvern Hill, shake his head and look for another way, another day.

But Lee thought differently. Lee, newly in charge, temporarily filling General Johnson's place, was feeling his oats. Lee felt, rightly, that he had rattled Mac's confidence. He had put the Union Army on the run. Malvern Hill was all that stood defending the main body of Mac's Army so that, by taking it, he could turn McClellan's orderly retreat into a rout.

At Gaines's Mill Porter fought without expecting to survive. At Malvern Hill he rested without expecting to fight. When Lee attacked,

The Fitz John Porter monument is the centerpiece of Haven Park, in Portsmouth, New Hampshire. The statue is positioned to salute a flag in front of Porter's birthplace, a house that Porter and his family left by the time he was five. Porter had only two memories, both traumatic, of Portsmouth. His father proved to be a disappointing member of the famous "Fighting Porters" naval family, incapable of commanding ships at sea or the Portsmouth Navy Yard, due to a drinking problem. After his father died when he was ten, Porter was raised by his mother, who never remarried. Both of his brothers went into the Navy while Porter, inexplicably, went to West Point and into the Army. (Original photo courtesy Doug Kerr)

Shortly after graduating eighth in his class at West Point, Porter served in combat as an artillerist. Knocked off his horse by a spent cannonball, Porter's Mexican War bas relief *is captioned, "Lt. F.J. Porter wounded at the Aqueduct, Garita Beléno, Capture of the City of Mexico, September 13, 1847." Kelly provided Porter with a scared horse, rearing back. The New York Historical Society holds Kelly's brief note dated March 4, 1901, "General I want to show a panel of you at the capture of Mexico City. Were you mounted at the time you were wounded? Yes." On the ground, Porter extends his right arm to touch the back of his head or neck. No American holds or fires a rifle. Porter's sword is in its scabbard. Kelly's focus is exclusively the wounded man. The shocked old veteran, a bearded soldier, his back a fine target for the enemy, who rushes forward unrealistically, his arms up in a gesture of dismay, is present only to direct a viewer's attention to the fallen figure, Porter wounded. (Original photo courtesy Doug Kerr)*

After Porter's knock-down (close up above), he rose, rode back to his unit, took command because his two superior officers were dead, and took over and loaded and fired a howitzer practically single-handed under continuous sniper fire until the major route into the capital of Mexico that he stood before, the Belén Gate, fell. On that day, September 13, 1847, the United States effectively won the war. (Original photo courtesy Doug Kerr)

General Porter took readily to the skies. He was the only high-ranking officer who regularly - over a hundred times - went up in a balloon to make sketches of Confederate defenses. His monument commemorates his most dangerous day aloft, when his balloon's tether snapped and Porter, at age 40, in uniform, had to drop his sketch pad and binoculars to scramble acrobatically, to reach an overhanging valve, in order to release gas slowly and descend. In the end, nonetheless, his descent was so rapid (he called it falling "like a lump of lead"), Porter was lucky that his basket hit a tent ridge-pole, breaking his fall, and he tumbled to the ground unhurt. (Original photo courtesy Doug Kerr)

James E. Kelly, the Brooklyn-born sculptor, worked from life, sketching both Porter and his binoculars, which survived the war in his possession. Kelly depicted a calm and cool man at the moment of scanning the rebel camp at besieged Yorktown in order to make a report to General McClellan, head of the Army of the Potomac. (Original photo courtesy Doug Kerr)

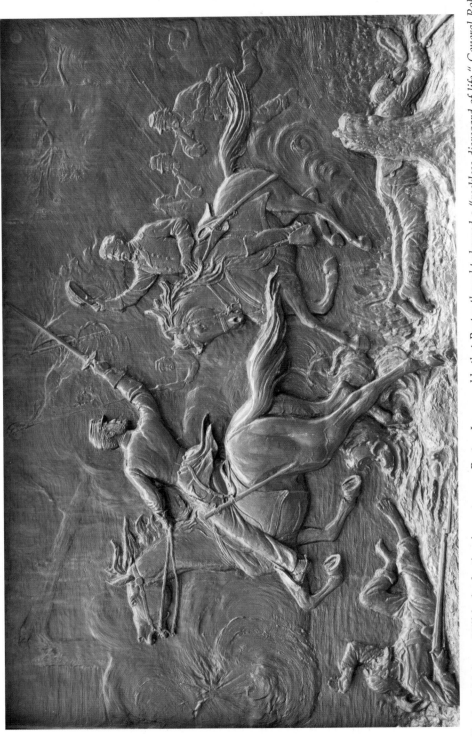

The Battle of Malvern Hill had a lasting impact upon Porter. In a gamble that Porter thought showed a "reckless disregard of life," General Robert E. Lee sent thousands of young men to die without any gain before Porter's hundred guns. Rebel troops, advancing uphill on an open field, were mown down "like rows of grass." A Confederate general, General D.H. Hill, said that "it was not war - it was murder." In Kelly's panel, General Thomas "Meagher of the Sword" Meagher takes off his cap in deference to Porter. (Original photo courtesy Doug Kerr)

D

The Battle of Malvern Hill took place on July 1, 1862 - the Porter monument was unveiled and dedicated on the horrific battle's anniversary, July 1, 1904. The date was set by terms of the bequest that funded the monument, given by Porter's admiring cousin, a patent lawyer named Robert H. Eddy. (Original photo courtesy Doug Kerr)

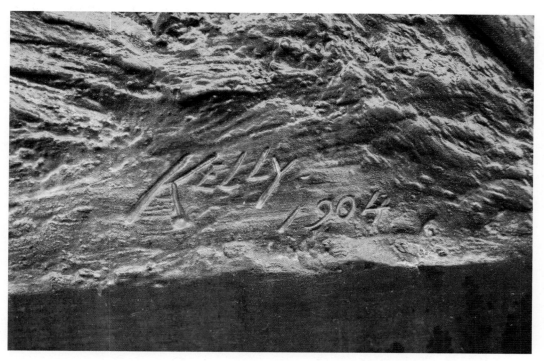

"Kelly 1904" is the signature of the sculptor, James E. Kelly, at the time the best-known sculptor of Civil War themes. Kelly's works stand at Gettysburg, in Yonkers and in museums. (Original photo courtesy Doug Kerr)

A barefoot, wounded rebel infantryman, terrified underfoot of Porter's horse, his weapon useless at his side, is probably screaming. Porter wrote of walking on the battlefield after the battle, where it was difficult not to step on the bodies of severely wounded rebels. (Original photo courtesy Doug Kerr)

A Confederate officer who died in his boots exemplifies the result of Lee's unwise order to charge at Malvern Hill. (Original photo courtesy Doug Kerr)

ON THIS SITE
WAS BORN
FITZ JOHN PORTER
AUG. 31, 1822
WHILE HIS FATHER
CAPT. JOHN PORTER, U.S.N.
COMMANDED THE PORTSMOUTH NAVY YARD.
GRADUATED FROM WEST POINT, JULY 1845
DISTINGUISHED HIMSELF AND WAS WOUNDED IN WAR WITH MEXICO
1846-1847.
INSTRUCTOR OF ARTILLERY AND CAVALRY
WEST POINT 1854-1855.
ASS'T. ADJ. GEN. UTAH EXPEDITION 1857.
DURING CIVIL WAR
BREV. BRIG. GEN. U.S.A. JUNE 27, 1862
MAJ. GEN. U.S. VOL. JULY 4, 1862
COMMANDED ✠ ARMY CORPS.
CASHIERED JAN. 21ST. 1863.

THE CASE OF GEN. PORTER WAS REVIEWED BY
A BOARD OF OFFICERS APPOINTED BY
PRESIDENT HAYES
CONSISTING OF
LIEUT. GEN. J. M. SCHOFIELD
BREV. MAJ. GEN. A. H. TERRY
BREV. MAJ. GEN. G. W. GETTY
HON. JOSEPH H. CHOATE COUNSEL FOR GEN. PORTER
THE BOARD FULLY EXONERATED HIM
THEIR JUDGMENT WAS APPROVED BY
GENERAL U.S. GRANT.
FINALLY BY BOTH HOUSES OF CONGRESS
HE WAS RESTORED TO HIS FORMER
RANK IN THE REGULAR ARMY
BY
PRESIDENT CLEVELAND

DIED AT MORRISTOWN, NEW JERSEY.
MAY 21ST. 1901.

The front tablet in words rather than images was agreed upon by the Porter family at Porter's home on Thanksgiving Day, 1900. Then and there, the idea of portraits of Porter's parents was discarded. Instead, the family wanted GENERAL U.S. GRANT's name prominently displayed. After Porter was court-martialed, Grant was an energetic, although very belated, convert to Porter's case for reinstatement to the Army. The full text of this tablet can be found on page 76.

Second Bull Run, the source of Porter's controversial status in American history, is neither depicted nor named anywhere on the tablet. Only the date of Porter's cashiering appears. A better choice, with sculpted figures, may have been August 29, 1862, the date that some, including the Schofield board that heard over a hundred witnesses, conclude that Porter saved not only his Fifth Corps but the Union Army itself at Second Bull Run. (Original photo courtesy Doug Kerr)

His Union cap over his heart,
Porter is saluting the flag. Besides
symbolizing patriotic motive, Kelly
thus indicates that Porter had a
secret in his breast but here, on this
monument, he was going to bare his
head and his heart to visitors. Porter
implicitly, as if in code, gave his
side of the story of Second Bull Run
on August 29, 1862, when he and
the 10,000 men of the Fifth Corps
stood in place and did not charge
the Confederates. (Original photo
courtesy Doug Kerr)

Attorney Robert H. Eddy, Porter's
cousin, had proposed in his will
that "Market Square or some other
conspicuous place" be the site for
the monument he funded. Public
opposition left Haven Park the only
alternative, across the road from the
house where Porter was born and
lived through a chaotic childhood
as part of a dysfunctional family.
(Original photo courtesy Doug Kerr)

H

Porter was shocked. Immediately galloping in front of his men, Porter fell heavily from his horse. Then, in what was the rarest of conditions for him, sheer, admitted panic, he ripped up his diary and his campaign notes. The confusion did not lift. When Porter authorized firing from gunboats, his own headquarters was shelled, with some casualties. Finally, at twilight, came waves of an uncoordinated Confederate charge.

Writing of the moment in his article for *Century*, Porter recalled that, around 5:30, after "an ominous silence intervened, the enemy opened up with artillery from nearly the whole of his front, and soon afterward pressed forward his columns of infantry. As if moved by a reckless disregard of life, with a determination to capture our army or destroy it by driving us into the river, regiment after regiment, and brigade after brigade, rushed at our batteries; but the artillery mowed them down with shrapnel, grape and canister, while our infantry scattered the remnants of their columns."

Confederate General D.H. Hill, his admiration turning into horror, wrote, "I never saw anything more grandly heroic than the advance after sunset of nine brigades but most of them had an open field half a mile wide to cross, under the fire of field-artillery in front, and the fire of the heavy ordnance of the gun-boats in their rear. It was not war—it was murder."

A Union infantryman likewise wrote home quoting an unnamed artillerist who "said that it made him heart sick to see how it cut roads through them some places ten feet wide." Soldiers at a distance heard clearly that Malvern Hill was an artillerist's fight. Corporal Mann, whose regiment came up the James River by steamboat too late to take part in the battle, reported its sounds in his diary: "booming cannon and fitful musketry."

After what Bruce Catton called "one of the most tragic and hopeless attacks of the war," Porter said that he "crossed a portion of the ground over which a large column had advanced to attack us, and had a fair opportunity of judging of the effect of our fire upon the ranks of the enemy."

As darkness fell, Porter discovered that "few steps could be taken without trampling upon the body of a dead or wounded soldier, or without hearing a piteous cry, begging our party to be careful." He thought of them as his "fellow countrymen" and their cries made him "deplore the effects of a fratricidal war." Behind Southern lines, the still-mesmerized D.H. Hill watched men go about with lanterns, looking for and carrying off the dead and wounded. Behind Northern lines, sanity was tested. Hennessy reported that, "during the night following Malvern Hill, Porter's fellow General Martindale suffered a spasm of panic and proposed the surrender of the army to the Confederates." Forsaking a graphic discussion, Porter the Victorian spoke of his reactions instead, "We gave what cheer we could to the wounded and left with heavy hearts."

Surprisingly, Porter's night was only beginning. The fight he won was followed by one he lost—with his friend, McClellan. Porter kept to the day he died that half-page order dated 9 p.m., July 1, 1862, in which General McClellan advised Porter that McClellan "desires you to move your command at once, the artillery reserve moving first to Harrison's Bar. In case you should find it impossible to move your heavy artillery, you are to spike the guns & destroy the carriages."

Malvern Hill was meaningless if Richmond did not fall. Richmond was what the Peninsula Campaign had been about. Malvern Hill, the last of its battles, was the source of unprecedented Confederate bloodletting. As noted by McPherson, "the thirty thousand men killed and wounded in the Seven Days' equaled the number of casualties in all the battles in the western theater—including Shiloh—during the first half of 1862." Confederate losses exceeded Union losses only because of Malvern Hill. Of Lee's 20,141 casualties, three-fourths came from Malvern Hill. On the night of July 1, 1862 Lee's army was more vulnerable than it would be again until 1865.

Knowing this, Porter bolted for his horse. Certain from his visit to the battlefield that Lee's ranks had been decimated, Porter rode to the James River, where McClellan rested on a gunboat, the *Galena*. Having survived his near-death experience, having heard the cries of the wounded and seen the bodies, Porter rose from his own fugue state to argue with his exhausted commander that the tide had turned, that they could now take Richmond, that this horrible war could end in 1862.

His daughter knew the story that her father never wrote.

"After the battle of Malvern Hill," Mrs. Doggett told Eisenschiml, "Father spent half the night with McClellan, trying to have him turn around and attack the Confederates before they could recover. But McClellan decided otherwise. Father always held that Richmond could have been taken right then and there."

A letter from General Alexander Stewart Webb confirmed Mrs. Doggett's tale as fact. Webb said that McClellan "sent word to Porter to spike his guns at the hour of victory and Porter went to McClellan on the gunboat and begged him to advance, but he would not."

McClellan was literally in no condition to listen. McClellan had just written Lincoln for fifty thousand more men, self-consciously rambling, saying, "I must apologize for the incoherency of this letter. I am exhausted by want of sleep and constant anxiety for many days." He wrote his wife, "I am completely exhausted—no sleep for days—my mind almost worn out." Perhaps sensing that McClellan was not himself, Porter never criticized him. Porter's article on Malvern Hill stops well short of recounting his argument to attack Richmond and McClellan's rejection of it.

Curiously enough, Stonewall knew McClellan's mind that night. As Donald Davis described, while Porter pled in vain with Mac, "concerned about a possible counterattack, Ewell and D.H. Hill went to try to awaken Jackson at one o'clock in the morning. With the help of aides, they managed to get him to sit up. Somewhere in the core of his brain, Jackson was still able to think beyond the smoke of cannons, the moans of the dying, and the desperate pleas of his field commanders. McClellan 'will clear out in the morning,' he predicted, and went back to sleep."

McClellan did clear out in the morning, and, after the retreat, heaped honors on Porter. He praised Porter and recommended his promotion. Cited for "chivalric and soldierly bearing under fire" at Malvern Hill, Porter was promoted to Major General of Volunteers and brevet Brigadier General in the Regular Army. McClellan's July 7, 1862 letter to Stanton read:

> The energy, ability, gallantry and good conduct displayed throughout the eventful period of this campaign by Brig. Genl. F.J. Porter, desires (*sic*) the marked notice of the Executive and the nation.
>
> If there were another grade to add I would ask for it for the battle of Malvern. The latter eclipsed in its results any other engagement in the campaign, and too much credit cannot be given to Genl Porter for his skill, gallantry, and conduct on the occasion.

I saw myself the dispositions he made and the gal-
lantry he displayed. I do not speak from hearsay, but from
personal observation; would that the country had more
General Officers like him.

Kelly depicted Malvern Hill as Porter greeting Meagher and, in a
twist one must confront, Kelly pictured "Meagher of the Sword" doffing
his hat to Porter. Interpreting this requires background facts. During the
war, Meagher was the personification of the bloody warrior. Currier &
Ives ran off a popular lithograph, "Meagher at the Battle of Fair Oaks,
Va. June 1st, 1862" over the extended caption, "The bayonet charge of the
Irish Brigade at this battle was the most stubborn, sanguinary and bloody
of modern times. Again and again they advanced with the cold steel, and
were as vigorously met by the enemy. In one place on the field of carnage,
three men were found on each side that had fallen by mutual thrusts. But
at last the battle terminated in favor of the Union arms, the Rebels gave
way in fight, and the victorious Army of the Potomac continued their
advance on Richmond." At Malvern Hill, on Kelly's panel, Meagher *defers
to Porter*. This totally imaginary scene was invented to illustrate Porter
as being mightier than the Sword. Likewise, at the bottom of the tablet,
a barefoot Confederate infantryman on his back fears Porter's trampling
horse. Obviously terrified, he raises his bare hand, his rifle useless beside
him. Near him, a better-clothed rebel has died with his boots on, having
fallen forward while advancing, lying face-down next to a shattered tree
stump. Put together, the slain and the wounded show, by Kelly's decision,
that nothing good or brave remained after Lee's murderous charge.

Malvern Hill really was such a bloodbath that Lee could have been
removed from command for it. Donald Davis noted that at Malvern Hill
"there were none of the grand movements, flanking gambits, or adroit
tactics for which Lee and Jackson are famous, just men blindly charging
up a steep hill." On the contrary, the Southern reaction was ecstasy.
Malvern Hill was the future and Jefferson Davis, speaking for a united
South, blessed it. Davis, a West Point graduate who had led the "Mississippi Rifles" to Mexico and had been the Secretary of War in President
Buchanan's cabinet, was President of the Confederate States of America.
Davis wrote Lee in admiration of how, "with well-directed movements
and death-defying valor, you charged upon the enemy in his strong
positions, drove him from field to field, over a distance of more than

thirty-five miles, and despite his reinforcements, compelled him to seek safety under cover of his gunboats, where he now lies cowering before the army so lately divided and threatened with entire subjugation." No Southern editor questioned Lee's orders at Malvern Hill or the necessity for so many casualties. Lee enjoyed broad and uncritical acclaim.

Porter was praised, too, although less publicly. McClellan wrote to his wife on July 27, 1862, that "Fitz John Porter has...struck through it all most nobly—he is all that I thought him & more. Nothing has depressed him; he is always cheerful, active & ready, & is much more efficient than all put together." And Porter's advice was valued. President Lincoln, who personally polled each one of McClellan's corps commanders during a visit to the army on July 8 and 9, 1862, paid Porter the honor of asking him six questions. The one that dealt with retreat each general answered differently. When he asked Porter, "If it were desired to get the army away from here, could it be safely effected?" Lincoln took down Porter's response in his own handwriting: "Impossible—move the Army & ruin the country."

Porter, disturbed by Malvern Hill, doubtless hopeful that the suicidal charge would remain a tactic limited to Lee and that Lee would abandon it before he lost too many more men, thought retreat was impossible. Porter stood his ground in support of a slow and steady strategy for victory.

Then came Pope.

6

Nemesis:
Porter and Pope to Second Bull Run, First Day

Created to conquer, aimed at Richmond and named for its target, the "Army of Virginia" was an invasion force of 70,000 men trained by McClellan but led by General John Pope. Its memorable battle, the Second Battle of Bull Run, was the battle intended to end all battles. At the end of the second day of battle, Pope even thought that he had won, and that Lee was in full retreat. Pope was wrong. After he lost, Pope needed someone to blame and Porter came to mind.

A military biographer sums Pope up in twenty-six words, "Pope strides abruptly into the center of things in 1862, captures Island No. 10, loses the Second Battle of Bull Run, and strides off into obscurity." But Pope's triumph at Island No. 10 in April, 1862 was a seeming marvel of the age. The editor of *Frank Leslie's Illustrated Magazine* asked, "Where, in the whole history of this country, or of modern warfare, can we point to results so grandly achieved without bloodshed?" Without casualties, his army captured Confederates in numbers that exceeded all earlier Union victories combined. After Island No. 10, Pope walked on water. It was only to be expected that Secretary of War Edwin Stanton would offer command of the Army of Virginia to Pope. Pope was not only a military hero but also an old friend of President Lincoln's, the fair-haired son of a judge before whom prairie lawyer Lincoln had practiced law, and related by marriage to Mary Todd Lincoln. What was not expected was Pope telling Stanton to his face, "I do certainly not view with any favor the proposition to place me in command." Pope said that he thought that he would be "in the situation of the strange dog, without even the right to run out of the village."

When Stanton reported Pope's answer to Lincoln, Lincoln cornered the strange dog in the White House and permitted him no escape. Pope accepted command of the new Army of Virginia on June 27, 1862, the day Porter was fighting for his life at Gaines's Mill. Pope recommended himself to his new command in the immortal words that were to haunt him later, "I have come to you from the West, where we have always seen the backs of our enemies," then showed his ego in an even scarier way. Pope challenged basic strategies, saying, "I hear constantly of taking strong defenses and holding them, of lines of retreat and of bases of supplies. Let us discard such ideas."

On July 29, 1862, Porter wrote to his surrogate father, Stephen M. Weld of Jamaica Plain, of having "no confidence in Pope." He was just being objective. Porter continued to be driven by duty and wrote his brother-in-law on August 12, 1862, "Of course I prefer McClellan to anyone but my loyalty to him does not deter me from giving all my efforts to anyone else. To crush the rebellion is my aim and to do it effectively and soon is my dearest wish." Porter must have expected by then that his Fifth

General John Pope was related to Lincoln by marriage. One of the four Army officers assigned to escort Lincoln during his train trip from Springfield to Washington for the Inauguration in 1861, Pope became the Union's best-loved instant hero in April, 1862 when he took a fort on the Mississippi without a single casualty. The Confederates simply surrendered besieged Island Number Ten. In July, Lincoln formed an army of 70,000 troops transferred from other commands, chiefly McClellan's Army of the Potomac. Naming the transfers the Army of Virginia, Lincoln gave them to Pope to lead to victory in Virginia. When Lee defeated Pope badly, that name was retired and survivors were assigned back to their original places. It was Pope who accused Porter of failing to obey his battlefield orders. (Photo courtesy of the Library of Congress; James Erik, http://JamesErik. com.)

Major General Fitz John Porter, and Staff

In early August yet to be transferred into Pope's Army of Virginia, Porter stands with his staff for a photograph. He had predicted to his aide, Lieutenant Weld, that the Union Army would have to win at Bull Run in order to take Richmond and end the war in 1862. He was correct on both points, but Pope's Army of Virginia did not win. Porter is near center, seated. (Photo courtesy of the Library of Congress; James Erik, http://JamesErik.com.)

Corps would be swept into the new army that would march without taking strong positions or retreating, while supply trains raced to catch up with it.

Pope and Porter met in Virginia, barely. They exchanged about as many words as politeness required and no more. In his memoirs Pope wrote about bumping into Porter at Pope's headquarters, "a most gentlemanlike man, of a soldierly and striking appearance. I had but little conversation with him, as I was engaged, as he was in writing telegrams." Pope tagged calm Porter for one-upmanship. Pope said that Porter "seemed to exhibit a listlessness and indifference not quite natural under the circumstances," an attitude Pope discounted as "not unusual for men to assume in the midst of dangers and difficulties merely to impress one with their superior coolness." But that was Porter.

The fiasco of Second Bull Run in a nutshell: It began when Stone-wall Jackson captured the Union supply depot at Manassas Junction on August 27. What the rebels did not eat or haul off, they burned. Lee planned that if that raid lured Pope to Bull Run, he would turn its familiar terrain into a Confederate shooting gallery. Pope took the bait, occupying Bull Run in force within two days. On August 29 Lee closed the trap with a rush of troops led by General Longstreet through the Thoroughfare Gap until, outnumbering Pope, they lay quietly in wait all that day behind an abandoned railroad embankment at the edge of Bull Run. Not seeing many rebels, presuming them to be in retreat, Pope declared victory that night in a triumphant telegram sent over the wire the next morning. He did not send a correction. He retreated on August 30 and, in person at the White House, gave Lincoln the details of Lee's greatest victory. According to Pope, who said that he had nothing against Porter, Porter was prosecuted because Lincoln wanted Porter prosecuted.

Among the corps ordered to hunt down Jackson, on August 27, Porter and the Fifth Corps arrived at Warrenton Junction, some fourteen miles from Manassas Junction, having marched, according to Eisenschiml, "steadily for two weeks, and on the last day without water and food." Beyond his supply lines, in the dark of the night of August 27-28, Porter received Pope's first order. Porter was to resume marching to Bristow Station at 1 a.m.

Porter convened a staff meeting. He stated the order and then he invited his officers to prove to him that execution of Pope's order was impossible. It was a pattern Porter would repeat when Pope ordered him to charge on the evening of August 29. Brigadier General Daniel Butterfield recalled how they "spoke with regard to the fatigue our troops had endured, the darkness of the night, and the fact that, in their judgment, the troops would be of more service to start at a later hour than they would be to start at the hour named. In reply to these remarks General Porter spoke rather decidedly, that there was the order; it must be obeyed; that those who gave the order knew whether the necessities of the case would warrant the exertions that had to be made to comply with it."

But when he took his officers outside of his tent, Porter found the night so dark that he told them, "In consideration of all the circumstances, I will fix the hour at 3 o'clock instead of one. You will be ready to move, promptly." Precedent had been set. A problem was in play. The first charge against Porter at his court-martial would be that he started out at 3 a.m. instead of 1 a.m. Stating Pope's order and then allowing proof that execution was impossible was a pattern Porter would repeat. When Pope ordered him to charge on the evening of August 29, that disobedience—by far the most serious charge against Porter—was likewise preceded by Porter first telling his staff that the order had to be obeyed and then, hearing reasons why success would be impossible, changing his mind. One wonders whether the one-two debating society pattern of "follow the insane order" followed by "it is an insane order, we cannot do it" was a charade performed for the record. It did not insulate Porter from prosecution or conviction—he remained in charge and responsible—but the pattern provided several witnesses to a rational defense, witnesses to obstacles presented at the time to Porter by third parties, while Porter on the record said, "An order is an order."

The 1 a.m. versus 3 a.m. start-time made no difference except that it allowed Porter's men a little extra sleep. When Porter arrived at Bristow Station in mid-morning on August 28, he found neither friend nor foe. The Fifth Corps stacked arms, made camp and awaited supplies and further orders—and supplies.

That afternoon, at about 4 o'clock, no supplies arrived but an officer did. Lieutenant Colonel Thomas C.H. Smith from Pope's headquarters dropped by to speak with Porter. It was hate at first sight. Smith wanted Porter to organize a search party for 300,000 rounds of ammunition. These were supply lines that Pope said would take care of themselves. They were Pope's, not his corps commanders' responsibility. Porter blandly replied to Smith that "he had no officers to take charge of it and to distribute it, or look it up, or something of that kind. I remarked that he could hardly expect us at headquarters to be able to send officers to distribute it in his corps; that it had been sent forward on the road in the direction where his corps was. He replied that it was going where it belonged; that it was on the road to Alexandria, where we were all going."

The excitable colonel rode back, hot and fuming, to Pope's headquarters, where he told Pope that Porter would fail him.

"How can he fail me?" Pope asked Smith, repeating a mantra with feeling, "He will fight where I put him, he will fight where I put him."

Smith angrily declared "that Fitz John Porter was a traitor; that I would shoot him that night, so far as any crime before God was concerned, if the law would allow me to do it."

With an incensed staffer ranting beside him, Pope dictated another order, that Porter move upon Centreville at the first dawn. The promised 300,000 rounds of ammunition might not have yet caught up with Porter—Smith could not tell—but Pope directed Porter to move upon Centreville, his supply trains to catch up later. Porter obeyed, marching his unfed men without supplies.

7

Second Bull Run, Second Day, August 29, 1862

Left unsupplied, Porter complained. At 6 a.m., August 29, as he was getting underway, Porter sent a telegram to General Ambrose Burnside, then his friend and confidant, complaining that forty wagons of supplies from Fort Monroe could not be found, that many animals had not been watered for fifty hours, and that he would be entirely out of provisions the next day. His truthful but negative updates were introduced at Porter's court-martial as evidence of the mind of a saboteur.

Indeed, to this day investigators of the military disaster take up Porter's pessimistic telegrams as a "black box" of records from which the cause of the Union crash at Second Bull Run may be explained. Among those seizing upon the telegrams to infer a broader military mindset, armchair generals Schutz and Trenberry in their military biography of Pope said, "If Porter had attacked when he should have, Jackson's line would have collapsed and Pope would have won his battle." For them, the cause of the lost battle was not Porter's inaction but "a tacit understanding among the Democrats of the Army of the Potomac not to allow Pope a victory."

But Porter knew the cause of the Pope's defeat. Porter's suspected agent of disaster was suspected by others, too. His nominee for villain was the subject of an inconclusive board of inquiry, although not a court-martial. The one who had briefly sat in the hot seat for his behavior during Second Bull Run, Porter's accused, was none other than General Irvin McDowell.

Historians still ask if General Irvin McDowell, pictured above, was the man most responsible for Union defeats at both First Bull Run in 1861 and Second Bull Run in 1862. Porter, after Second Bull Run, identified McDowell as the cause of that bloody defeat and ignominious Union retreat. A court-martial, however, blamed Porter. The Schofield Board later exonerated Porter while it criticized McDowell as well as the man in command of Porter and McDowell, General John Pope. (Photo courtesy of the Library of Congress; James Erik, http:// JamesErik.com.)

Porter wrote, "Pope was defeated because Longstreet was let to come through Thoroughfare Gap on the morning of August 29." McDowell inexcusably abandoned his post at the Gap. General Abner Doubleday, himself at the Gap that night, wrote, "I never could quite understand why McDowell left us on that occasion, especially as Hatch—whose brigade escorted him part of the way—says McDowell pointed out the position of the enemy before he left, and advised him to be *prepared for an attack.*" McDowell apparently decided that Pope needed his expertise more than the men at the Gap needed his supervision. When a dispatch rider from Major John Buford's cavalry caught up with McDowell the next morning, his news should have ended McDowell's career: masses of Confederates were pouring through the Gap unopposed.

McDowell met Porter shortly afterward. He displayed the Buford dispatch without comment, then slipped it back into his coat pocket just as Pope's joint order to McDowell and Porter arrived. The dean of Second Bull Run scholars, John J. Hennessy, called this order "a masterpiece of contradiction and obfuscation." Pope's unintelligible order to the two generals finally featured the sentence, "If any considerable advantages are to be gained by departing from this order it will not be strictly carried out."

McDowell, the senior of the two, claimed that he promptly told Porter, "You put your force in here, and I will take mine up the Sudley Springs road on the left of the troops engaged at that point with the enemy." On the contrary, officers on Porter's staff heard McDowell say distinctly, "Porter, you are too far out; this is no place to fight a battle."

Porter's daughter told Eisenschiml something even more explosive.

"When McDowell rode up to Father near Dawkins' Branch," she said, "he told him that McClellan's removal had been decided on, that he, McDowell, was going to play an important role in the army, and that those who were willing to join his side would not regret it. And do you know what Father replied? He was not going to let anyone run down McClellan in his presence, his fidelity was not for sale, and from then on he would talk to McDowell only on official business."

Porter himself only wrote that while "the enemy's return shots of our skirmishers or shots aimed at us were whizzing about," he and McDowell rode together in near-silence "to examine the character of the country." Porter emphasized cryptically that "very few words passed between us, neither feeling towards the other any desire to talk (certainly I did not), we rode in almost silence."

When, suddenly, McDowell snapped the reins of his horse and began to gallop away, Porter shouted after his departing senior, "What should I do?"

McDowell gestured "waved his hand and went on" leaving Porter to chase him with couriers sent for further orders while the Fifth

Corps spent the day in "enforced quietude." Astonishingly, by one of the great ironies of the Civil War, *quietude* was the single militarily correct thing for Porter to do on August 29. Quietude in place was exactly what stymied Lee.

During the war, McDowell damned Porter for his insubordination. After the war, McDowell finally conceded Porter's discretion.

In his official report after the battle on November 6, 1862, McDowell claimed that he "decided for Porter to throw himself at once on the enemy's flank." He testified the next month at Porter's court-martial that he left Porter with a positive order to attack the enemy at once.

Long after the war, in the witness-stand, under Joseph Choate's cross-examination before the Schofield board, McDowell wavered. He said that he had expected Porter to make decisions among options that included *declining battle*.

Attorney Choate's questions and McDowell's answers follow:

Q. Then a skirmish line would have answered your expectation when you left General Porter, if in his discretion that was more advisable?

A. It would depend upon the nature of the skirmish—how it was done; how vigorously carried out; whether the circumstances required it, and it only. It depends upon a great many things, that you must make a great many suppositions about, before I can give an intelligent answer. If you want to know a general principle, I believe it is laid down by military writers, that a body of men should be in a condition to offer battle or decline it; whether the main body shall be advanced or retire on the reserve, and many other positions; all of which are conditions upon which battles are determined.

Q. And determined upon the discretion of the corps commander?

A. Yes; provided he acted energetically.

Q. Provided he acted according to the best of his discretion as a soldier?

A. Yes, sir.

Q. Now I ask you, if, after making efforts necessary for the purpose, Porter had ascertained there was a force there double his own, after you left him and took King away, do you say he should have attacked?

A. He should have made an attack, yes.

Q. He should have made an attack just as you ordered it?

A. My order was, I confess to you, a very vague one. It was made to a person whose zeal and activity and energy I had every knowledge of—I did not pretend to give him any particular instructions or directions that he should skirmish, or shell, or charge, or anything of the sort; I merely indicated the direction in which his troops should be applied. Further than that I did not think and would not think now if I had the thing to go over again to direct.

With McDowell's wave of his hand as their last communication, Porter was suddenly without General Rufus King's men, almost a third of Porter's force, men whom McDowell took with him. In limbo, without communication, Porter felt "bound to his place till untied by orders from General Pope, or by knowledge of McDowell's arrival at or near his destination." The theoretical option of "moving at his will to risk disaster to the army and ruin to himself" sounded insane to Porter, the sanest of generals.

But standing in place bore fruit. The presence of the Fifth Corps's remaining 10,000 men flummoxed the rebels. Porter held Lee back from attacking. Confederate General Longstreet wrote a letter to General Grant confirming that, published after the war in the *Chicago Tribune*. Longstreet recalled that on August 29 "General Lee indicated his purpose to have me attack. Intending to execute his plan, I asked time to reconnoiter a new position and the ground intervening. After reconnaissance I reported the position strong, and that the sacrifice was likely to be such as to cause an apprehension of failure. He did not seem satisfied, and was considering the propriety of making his orders more definite when information was received from General Stuart of the approach of Federal troops upon my right."

Hennessy concluded in his book that "Lee's proposed counter-attack was stymied by Porter's presence." More specifically, according to Hennessy, Porter required Lee to extend Longstreet's line to the right and forced Lee to keep two brigades of cavalry along the Manassas-Gainesville road, maneuvers that drew the rebels' front far from the left of Pope's main body.

Porter, obviously ignorant of this rebel strategizing, had no better knowledge of the Union strategy. Lieutenant Weld testified at Porter's court-martial as the key witness of Porter's isolation from his superiors, Pope and McDowell. Weld started at about 4 o'clock in the afternoon of the 29th with a written message, General Porter gave him verbal messages as well that General Morrell would be strongly engaged, that there was a large force in front of him and that large clouds of dust were seen, indicating a host of Confederates.

At Pope's headquarters, Weld found McDowell first. McDowell read the dispatch and said, "I am not the man; there is the man," pointing to General Pope. Weld went up to General Pope and delivered the messages, both written and oral.

"I asked him whether he had any answer for General Porter," Weld testified. "He said, 'Tell General Porter we are having a hard fight.' Just then General Pope called General McDowell back. I asked him if that was all he had to send to General Porter, and he said, 'yes.' He then said to General McDowell, 'The enemy are trying to turn our right: they have sent one or two brigades there, and I want you to send your division.' General McDowell, as far as I can remember, made some objection, but General Pope insisted upon having a division sent there."

Incredibly, at the court-martial, Pope and McDowell simply and successfully denied having received Weld at all. The court-martial did not infer the obvious, that Porter received no messages from late morning, when McDowell rode off, until 4:30 or sunset. The assembled generals took the word of two generals over the word of one lieutenant.

Porter said that, before Weld, he had sent messages until he ran out of messengers. At about sunset, Porter finally got an order, one alternatively called "the 4:30 order" for the time of its dictation or "the sunset order" for the time of its receipt. Nobody could tell when it was given to its courier, Captain Douglas Pope, General Pope's nephew. Captain Pope testified to his prompt delivery of the order. He estimated that it was in Porter's hands no later than five-fifteen. Unfortunately for Pope, before the Schofield board, Choate later located two witnesses, Lieutenant Jones and Captain Moale, to whom Captain Pope admitted at the time that he had gotten lost for an hour or two while on the way to Porter.

In his memoirs, Porter himself described the time he got the order "near dark—when I saw coming towards me from the direction of Manassas a mounted officer unattended by any escort or orderly. That officer delivered to me the 4:30 p.m. order.

"I at once acknowledged in writing the receipt of the order and specified the hour of receipt.

"I then had a gold-plated watch with gold hands and so dark was it—we being surrounded by high trees—that I had to light a match to see the hour."

He blanked on the time he saw in the light of his match.

Porter's first response was to obey. Porter said that upon receiving the sunset order he "gave the order to attack and went to the front to see to it." Porter sent three orders in rapid succession with no times jotted down on any of them. The first order (hereafter, "No. 1") required General Morrell to make a reconnaissance. The second (hereafter. "No. 2") ordered him to be ready for battle. The third (hereafter, "No. 3") was the attack order. The messengers arrived in a different order. General Morrell received No. 1, then No. 3 and, "on receiving No. 2 concluded that No. 3 was countermanded and continued moving his troops into line to pass the night." Arriving at the front, Porter found such confusion and darkness that he called off the charge. As on the dark night of August 28, when he started the march to Bristow Station at 3 a.m. instead of 1 a.m., Porter began with insistence that an insane order was to be obeyed, followed by acceptance of his staff's reasoned case for non-compliance.

At court-martial, Porter was also accused of doing nothing although knowing that ferocious fighting was going on near him all day. His opponents argue that Porter was aware of a hard-fought battle but chose to sit out Pope's almost-successful campaign. In response to this charge, Choate had many veterans come forward to disprove any Fifth Corps' awareness of a general battle. Captain Augustus P. Martin, chief of artillery in Morrell's division of the Fifth Corps, said that he heard "skirmish firing only" on the 29th, no sounds that indicated a furious battle raging on his right. "Not the slightest," he said, "My recollection is clear. I have the fact so recorded in my diary, and my diary makes it perfect as far as my memory goes. If there was any it was beyond our hearing." General Charles Griffin testified that he "heard no firing whatever, except artillery at a long distance. That is, I can call to mind no other firing. In the evening a little after dark there were some heavy volleys of musketry, the enemy evidently driving our troops right before them. That musketry was to our right and front, I should say two miles, may be not so far; may be further. I should have stated. When I stated that I heard no other firing but artillery, that in marching we had (*sic*) some skirmish firing." Two miles closer to gunfire than Porter, General John Reynolds corroborated:

> Q. On the 29th, before 4 o'clock p.m., what was the character of the battle—artillery or infantry?
>
> A.: Principally artillery.
>
> Q.: About what time did the infantry fire commence in force and volume?
>
> A.: As near as I can recollect it must have been between 4 and 5 o'clock, probably 5 o'clock, that is, I refer to the part near me. There may have been infantry firing on the right which I could not hear.
>
> Q.: Was there not considerable and heavy infantry firing about 11 o'clock a.m. on the 29th, and at intervals from that time to 3 o'clock p.m.?
>
> A.: There was some firing intervals, but I do not recollect any very heavy infantry firing.

8

Second Bull Run, Third Day, and Beyond

As the third and worst day of Second Bull Run dawned, Pope's triumphant dispatch went humming over the wires to Washington. One of McDowell's staffers, a Lieutenant Roebling, wrote in his journal:

> Aug. 30. Day broke cloudy. Everything quiet. Not a shot was heard for some hours. We all met at Pope's Headquarters. Pope was bragging and over-confident (*sic*) . . . The enemy kept silent. Presently the idea gained ground that the enemy were (*sic*) retreating. In fact, Pope was very sanguine that they had retreated, and commenced to make arrangements about putting a column in pursuit.

Pope, his army and its animals hungry and thirsty, most of his supplies thirty miles away in Alexandria or stalled on wagon-choked roads between Alexandria and Manassas, was in denial. Colonel Frederick T. Locke testified to this battle as "the only time in his life when he felt the cravings of hunger." Captain John Piatt, an aide-de-camp of General Pope, testified that on the 29th "the body guard made some coffee in the field, and gave me a cup of coffee. That is all I had to eat."

Pope, who retained authority over 70,000 men, wherever their supplies were, ordered Porter to come to him.

Lee immediately noticed. Lee got his break. When Porter arrived at the main body, Pope ordered him to work on Jackson's forces. Porter sent out an initial force. To draw the Union soldiers into deeper jeopardy,

Stonewall allowed them to meet with some success. At about 11 a.m. on August 30, Porter's forward skirmishers returned with a wounded Union soldier who claimed to have heard the rebel officers say their army was retiring to unite with Longstreet. Porter sanely feared a trap. He sent the soldier on to Pope along with a warning about the man, "I regard him either as a fool or designedly released to give a wrong impression and no faith should be put in what he says."

Pope sent back a courier to Porter with the message, "General Pope believes that soldier and directs you to attack."

Porter made preparations while, unknown to him, on the ridge to his rear, suspicious Pope furtively watched his movements. Had Porter not charged on August 30, Pope said grimly, "it would have been fatal to him personally."

But Pope had no need to shoot Porter.

When Porter attacked Jackson *en masse*, even Jackson was taken aback. During fighting so fierce that some of his men, out of ammunition, were reduced to gathering and throwing rocks, Jackson barely held back Porter's corps. For the first and only time during the war, Jackson sent to Longstreet for reinforcements. But when Stonewall asked for reinforcements, Stonewall got reinforcements. Longstreet's army, the very one that Pope thought had retreated, suddenly appeared, 25,000 strong, the largest simultaneous assault of the war by either side. Nothing like it faced Meade at Gettysburg nor Grant in any of his battles. It was completely unexpected by Pope, who refused to believe the first reports of what was happening. General John F. Reynolds, the general captured along with Lieutenant Weld during the Seven Days' battles and with Weld in the batch of officers exchanged just before Second Bull Run, rode through hellish fire and shells to convince Pope that disaster was on the march. Reynolds had to play Paul Revere before the Union Army lurched into retreat over the bridge across Bull Run. Instantly, it became Porter's job to serve as rear guard. The enemy saw the backs of Pope's army. With bitter irony, the line of retreat that Pope had spurned as a tactic to be discarded turned out to be useful after all.

Porter's outnumbered and exhausted troops fought as if in a trance, keeping up a steady fire. One of them, the same Corporal Mann who used to watch Porter up in a balloon, said that as his comrades were falling around him, "I was not excited. Let me tell you the reason. *I expected to die.*" Walt Whitman's brother, G.W. Whitman, wrote home that August 30th was "about as sharp a fight as I ever wish to see." Porter's brave men, within range of Confederate artillery, dropped back first to Chinn Ridge, then to Henry House Hill, where Porter linked up with General Reynolds before his survivors were the last to leave the battlefield. Porter's men were valiant beyond the call of duty that day but their deeds were forever unsung, obscured then as now in the Union defeat.

Soon after the battle, the two men met. Pope's Chief of Staff, General Ruggles, was present when they talked during the retreat at Fairfax Court-House, then Pope's headquarters, on September 2. Ruggles wrote that:

> General Porter and General Pope had a conversation lasting about 20 minutes. I think there was nobody else in the room except myself. Whilst studiously avoiding overhearing the conversation I heard scraps. At the conclusion of the interview General Pope and General Porter got up and I heard General Pope say to General Porter that his explanations were satisfactory with the exception of the matter of one brigade. I knew the matter of the one brigade meant Griffin's brigade from my knowledge of what had happened at that time.

When Pope brought up Porter's dispatches to General Burnside, Pope said that Porter seemed surprised but explained. Apparently taking up one of the dispatches, he told Pope that it was a private letter to General Burnside and "expressed his regret that he had written the letter." Pope said that he thought he would take no further action. Pope said in a public memoir later, "I said so because I did not at that time believe that General Porter deliberately and of purpose had withheld his command from the assistance of the army engaged in that battle although I had been warned that he would fail me."

But it was hardly so. In his September 3 official report on the battle, Pope had obviously chosen his scapegoat, raging that "if the corps of Porter had attacked the enemy on the flank on the afternoon of Friday, August 29, as he had my 4:30 order to do, we should have crushed Jackson before the forces under Lee could have reached him. Why he did not do so I cannot understand."

During the court-martial, Pope disclaimed any prejudice against Porter and claimed that President Lincoln had persuaded him that Porter was culpable. Pope said that when he came to Washington on the fourth or fifth of September, he was informed by the President of General Porter's dispatches from Bull Run to General Burnside. "This opened my eyes to many matters which I had been loath to believe, and which I cannot bring myself now to believe," Pope said. Before the court-martial, Pope added archly, "The reason why I told Porter at Fairfax courthouse that I thought I should take no further action, was that I was inclined to think that his action or his want of action was the result of blundering rather than intention."

Pope's story, which signaled to the court-martial judges that the President had turned against Porter, was not exposed as fiction until he and Porter were both dead, when Gideon Welles' diary was published in 1911. Welles, Lincoln's Secretary of the Navy and a participant, wrote contemporaneously of their White House meeting on September 4:

> When with the President, this A.M., heard Pope read his statement of what had taken place in Virginia during the last few weeks, commencing at or before the battle of Cedar Mountain. It was not exactly a bulletin nor a report, but a manifesto, a narrative, tinged with wounded pride and a keen sense of injustice and wrong. The draft, he said, was rough. It certainly needs modifying before it goes out, or there will be war among the generals, who are now more ready to fight each other than the enemy. No one was present but the President, Pope, and myself. I remained by special request of both to hear the report . . .
>
> Pope and I left together and walked to the Departments. He declares all his misfortunes are owing to the persistent determination of McClellan, Franklin, and Porter, aided by Ricketts, Griffin, and some others who were determined that he should not be successful. They preferred, he said, that the country should be ruined rather than he should triumph.

Pope boasted of prosecuting Porter before the Committee on the Conduct of the War in 1865, saying, "I considered it a duty I owed to the country to bring Fitz-John Porter to justice, lest at another time, and with greater opportunities, he might do that which would be still more disastrous."

Other sources agree that Lincoln held no bad opinion of Porter to share with Pope. William A. Newell, a New Jersey politician who had served in the Congress with Lincoln, called on Lincoln in late 1864 asking about Porter's case. Newell said that "Mr. Lincoln stated that he had not been able to give that personal attention to the case which its merits required; that he had accepted the opinion of the Judge Advocate and of the War Department as the basis of his action…that he had a high regard for General Porter personally and as a soldier, and that he hoped that he would be able to vindicate himself."

Lincoln's high opinion of Porter in 1862 was also corroborated by an officer standing nearby when Lincoln took his leave of Porter on October 1 of that year. The officer recalled that Lincoln shook Porter's hand, "walked aside, and said to Porter, 'General, I cannot sufficiently thank you for your total self-abnegation and attention to your duties. I have marked them, and your gallant service will ever be remembered. I have been your friend in the past and, General, you can depend upon me for the future.'"

The Battle of Fredericksburg took place while Porter awaited trial. Although Porter had foreseen disastrous casualties, he was not honored as a prophet by his country. John Bigelow, an artillery Captain from New York, wrote home on November 10, 1862 news that McClellan had been removed in favor of Burnside, adding, "Fitz John Porter says there will not be nine effective men out of fifteen at the end of this campaign. It seems to be the general opinion that we shall meet with nothing but reverses." Likely reflecting Porter's attitude after the horrendous battle, Lieutenant Weld wrote his mother about Fredericksburg on December 17, 1862, "Just think, 15,000 wounded and killed, and no advantage gained or corresponding loss inflicted on the enemy!" Years later, on sending a map of Fredericksburg to a veteran named Edwin B. Robins, Porter wrote of his former confidant Burnside with undisguised contempt. Porter told Robins that the map "will give you the names and location of the streets up which you marched in obedience to Gen. Burnside's idiotic and murderous order." Hard war was not Porter's way of war. Charges into an entrenched enemy were a last resort.

Even Lee seemed to come to be wary of that way of warfare. At Fredericksburg on December 13, 1862, putting down the telescope through which he watched the massacre at "Burnside's Bridge," Lee told an aide, "It is well that war is so terrible, lest we grow too fond of it." Lee at Fredericksburg was in Porter's position at Malvern Hill. Belatedly, the Union's futile bloody frontal assaults seemed to exert the same horrible pull on Lee as Lee's futile charges had on Porter at Malvern Hill. One military historian wrote that "close examination of Lee's tactical thought from Fredericksburg until the end of the war indicates that he used the frontal assault only when he believed he had the advantage of surprise or had no other choice. Never, after Fredericksburg, did he accept the frontal assault as a feasible method to defeat an entrenched and ready enemy."

Stephen Sears noted that "the six weeks following Fredericksburg were a time of crisis in the Army of the Potomac, remembered ever after as the Valley Forge of its existence." Burnside offered his resignation, Lincoln returned it without comment, "McClellanism" was the catchall category for whatever interfered with fighting, and Porter, McClellan's favorite corps commander, was tried on charges.

Porter had decided to leave the Army. Porter, who had begun as a cadet at West Point in 1842, who had fought with unsurpassed bravery during the Mexican War, who had been willing to sacrifice himself and his command in June to take Richmond, who had told Lincoln in July not to retreat, whom the President had personally commended in October, who had known nothing but the Army life since turning twenty, was done with it all. He wrote his wife on December 12, 1862, "The feelings of the court is such that I believe their minds were made up long since. The administration is resolved upon dismissing me. I have been informed that members of the Cabinet have used their influence on members of the court. *I intend to resign, even if found not guilty.*"

Porter apparently confided his intention to resign to Lieutenant Weld. On December 30, Weld wrote to his father saying that he could not see how Porter could help being acquitted but added, "In any case, the general will see that I get a staff appointment. I had a talk with him this morning in which he said he would look out for me. I think if from any cause or reason he should not be in the service, that I shall try and get on General Reynolds's staff."

John Hay, Lincoln's private secretary, considered Porter "the most magnificent soldier in the Army of the Potomac." But Porter, who lacked the capacity for excitement, whose forte was imperviousness to panic, whose bland, intelligent personality had made him a good secret agent before hostilities began at Sumter, whose sane way of limited war had become a walking liability, was in the gun sights of higher authorities.

Because he told Colonel Smith the truth in a matter-of-fact tone during the afternoon of August 28, because he made a sane decision in the face of an insane order on August 29, ranking loyalty to Pope below saving lives, Porter was a marked man.

Porter summarized that he was "convicted of willfully refusing to obey orders; of refraining from giving battle in aid of his brother-soldiers; of neglecting to aid in achieving a success, the failure to gain which caused the loss of the lives of thousands of men, with woeful disaster to his country." His guilty verdict on all charges and sentence of cashiering was approved by President Lincoln on January 21, 1863 and was made public the following day. Lincoln seemed to have finally signed the sentence to punish his erstwhile favorite, Porter, based on his own ears. Porter's prosecutor, Kentucky-born Joseph Holt, told the story. Holt recalled his conference on the Porter case in the White House. While Holt had filled in briefly as President Buchanan's Secretary of War, he was no military man but a lawyer. Then trying his first case as Judge Advocate General with an *ex officio* rank of colonel, Holt met with two other non-military men, also lawyers by profession—Lincoln and his Secretary of War, Stanton. Holt said

> I read my review of the law and the testimony in the Porter case to President Lincoln and Mr. Stanton. My interview with those two men was very impressive. I read my review slowly and carefully, Lincoln and Stanton frequently interrupting with questions and references to the testimony.
>
> I was surprised to find how perfectly familiar the President was with the proceedings and the testimony and I expressed my astonishment that in the midst of his great cares, he had been able to read it all so carefully. He had followed the proceedings from day to day during the session. When I read that portion of the case which indicates that Porter must have known that Pope's Army was being driven from the sound of the artillery, Lincoln stopped me and said, "I distinctly heard that Battle from the southern windows of the War Department and I knew that the Army was retreating from the sound of the guns."

Thus fortified by his own knowledge, Lincoln interrupted Holt and hastily approved Porter's conviction and cashiering.

President Lincoln was Porter's war-time judge as Commander-in-Chief. Lincoln signed Porter's court-martial verdict and sentence only after he was satisfied, from what he had heard with his own ears from a window at the War Department, that Second Bull Run was a loud, furious fight in which anybody inactive must have been certainly guilty of disloyalty. (Photo courtesy of the Library of Congress; James Erik, http:// JamesErik.com.)

A century and a half too late to inform Lincoln or to help Porter, *Acoustic Shadows* by physicist Charles D. Ross came out and explained how the ears can be deceived and how commanders were tricked into both successes and failures during several Civil War battles. At Second Bull Run, not a battle Ross chose to analyze, the general principle he described would have applied: depending upon topographical features, sounds travel differently. For example, the sounds of artillery may be blocked or "shadowed" and go muffled or unheard *nearby* while, traveling down a "sound corridor," they are clearly audible at *a great distance.*

Unaware of sound corridor theory, Lincoln, who heard the guns of a great battle on August 29, condemned Porter on the basis of rumbles. Those present at Second Bull Run, like the foreign observer, the Count of Paris, heard sounds of artillery in the Fifth Corps' sector "like those artillery duels, to whose noise neither officer nor soldier used to pay attention in Virginia." The Schofield board wrote, "No sound but that of artillery was heard by Porter during all those hours when Porter was understood by the court-martial to have been listening to the sounds of a furious battle raging immediately to his right. And those sounds of artillery were by no means such as to indicate a general battle." In other words, what Lincoln heard with his own ears deceived him.

Even so, sound evidence was not the only factor. Lincoln's secretary, John G. Nicolay, wrote in his diary on January 23, 1863 of the political necessity behind Porter's conviction:

> Nothing of interest except the trial and dismissal of Major General Fitz-John Porter.
>
> *Whatever may be the justice of his sentence,* I have no doubt the result of the trial will have a salutary influence on the discipline and morale of the Army, teaching the officers that the principle of accountability to the Government is not yet obsolete.

9

The Cashiered General

Lee dismissed Porter as "a man who might do well enough, with someone else to tell him what to do," but the irony was that Porter thwarted Lee at Second Bull Run because there, when somebody *did* tell him what to do, he did *not* do it. Lee, anxious to destroy Pope, had fretted, raising and lowering his telescope all afternoon on August 29, 1862, while only Porter's corps blocked his path. Porter received Pope's order near sunset to charge headlong through a hilly field crowded with stumps and underbrush into Longstreet's rested and ready lines of marksmen. Rejecting it, Porter saved not only his corps but the main body of Pope's army. As 1863 began, Lee was probably glad that his troublesome former adjutant had been cashiered.

The cashiered soldier, Porter, got up after he fell, kept falling and kept getting up. First, Porter went to Colorado in 1864 to run a mining operation until a bill was introduced by the territorial legislature to expel him. During this period, his wife noticed that people she knew crossed the street when they saw her coming. The Porters considered exile, going to Europe and finding work there, but, networking through other contacts, Porter returned east for a temporary job supervising the construction of a new insane asylum in Morristown, New Jersey. When he was invited to fill out the unexpired term of the New York City Commissioner of Public Works, the Board of Aldermen promptly objected to him personally. Thrown out of that job, Porter left to serve the Central Railroad of New Jersey as its Assistant Receiver, probably a position he owed to his old commander, McClellan, the former railroad president and New Jersey

*The best lawyer of his time, and possibly ever, Joseph Choate,
was born on Hog Island, off the coast of Salem, Massachusetts.
Choate graduated Harvard Law School, after which joined a
small law firm in New York City which prospered. Largely upon
his skills, it became the largest and most profitable law firm
in New York. An anglophile, Choate became a most popular
ambassador to Great Britain. But, before departing for the Court
of Saint James, Choate brilliantly and successfully defended
Porter before the Schofield board, a Presidential fact-finding
commission. Porter gratefully placed Choate's name on the front
of his monument in Portsmouth. (Photo courtesy of the Library
of Congress; James Erik, http://JamesErik.com.)*

resident. Uncomfortable in a job created for him, Porter was attracted to
another New York City position, as police commissioner, despite its guar-
anteed unpopularity and notoriously short longevity. One must admire
the sane combination of methodical habits, self-discipline and resilience

that Porter exhibited in supporting his family. The series mirrors the adaptability he showed in the Army before the war, firing a howitzer in Mexico, teaching at West Point, bringing order to Kansas and Mormon country, consulting on confidential operations at the highest level in Washington, and running dangerous secret missions himself. Consider the adaptability of a man who took on jobs running a gold mine in Colorado, a huge public building under construction, a metropolitan public works and police department, even humbly performing a minor role in a railroad's financial arm.

Through it all, the working man, husband and father never forgot his case. He targeted the best trial lawyer in the country, Joseph Choate. Choate thought that he was guilty. Six times fall, seven times get up. Porter asked Choate to take the case *only if he were convinced of his innocence.* Then he left his paperwork for Choate to review.

Choate took the case.

Joseph Choate, whose name is emblazoned on the front tablet of Porter's monument, scoured the country, North and South, for survivors to supplement the war-time record. Choate's witnesses outnumbered the government's witnesses by better than two-to-one, 99 to the government's 43. It was also Choate's genius to choose the correct issue, not to challenge the charge of factual inaction on August 29 but strictly to develop why Porter had been right not to charge. Choate made the Schofield board understand Porter's heart and mind.

What Choate showed with maps and witnesses, Theodore Lord illustrated by way of a schematic. Lord showed Pope's errors in two neat diagrams or schematic maps:

WHAT POPE THOUGHT THE SITUATION WAS

	JACKSON
PORTER	22,000 men
10,000 men	POPE
	33,000 men

WHAT THE SITUATION ACTUALLY WAS

LONGSTREET	JACKSON
25,000 men	22,000 men
PORTER	POPE
10,000 men	33,000 men

Choate turned Porter's rehearing into a trial of Pope *in absentia*. It was a huge gamble because Pope might at any time appear and testify, perhaps well enough to salvage himself and stigmatize Porter. Throughout the trial, Choate kept one eye fixed on Pope, in distant California. Choate wrote home jubilantly on June 29, 1878, "Genl. Pope has concluded not to put in an appearance," but his news was premature. Pope angled for a subpoena but the advisory board possessed no subpoena power. Then he looked for orders to appear from superiors who were unwilling to issue them. Accordingly, the anxious Choate was finally relieved to write his wife on October 24, 1878, "Well, I got word today that Genl. Pope refuses to come. Nothing so good could possibly happen for Genl. Porter's cause."

With the record closed, the Schofield board held unanimously that *Porter* as cause of the loss of Second Bull Run had been disproved. Implicitly, *Pope* was the source of the catastrophe. The board's report made headlines all across the country. Porter did not jump up and down or cry tears of joy. His daughter recalled that her father took the news quietly, showing no emotion. As Porter knew, to reverse his sentence required an Act of Congress and the President.

People rose up to discredit the board's report, including veterans of the war. The General to whom Porter had confided in telegrams from Second Bull Run, Ambrose Burnside, was among his opponents now. Burnside, criticized by Porter for having ordered ten thousand men to die in a futile assault on "Burnside's Bridge" at Fredericksburg, sarcastically disagreed that Porter had rendered great service "in saving the Union Army from destruction" because he was:

> forced to say that he does not know exactly what would have happened to the Union Army had General Porter not remained quiet all the day of the 29th of August or had he obeyed the order given him to attack, because he is not possessed of the high order of military intelligence which would enable him to derive exactly what the enemy would have done.

In his analysis of the Schofield board Burnside, to give him his due, accurately noted that "some of the so-called 'fundamental errors' of the court-martial which the board have summed up in a few words are not errors of fact." But Burnside was not a lawyer. As Choate the lawyer

General Schofield, head of the Army, was selected by President Rutherford B. Hayes to chair a board of three, including the Army's two other top generals. President Hayes commissioned them to find and report to him the truth about what happened at Second Bull Run, whether Porter was guilty as charged of cowardice under fire on August 29, 1862. The Schofield board exonerated Porter. (Photo courtesy of the Library of Congress; James Erik, http://JamesErik.com.)

knew, inferences are precisely where most cases are won or lost. The difference between the court-martial and the Schofield board was basically their respective inferences and projections from similar facts.

James Garfield, a court-martial-member soon to be President, declined to exonerate or to excuse Porter after the Schofield board's hearings and report and even wanted to go to court to defend the validity of the court-martial verdict. He stopped because he found, upon inquiring, that he lacked legal standing. But Garfield, Burnside, other vocal Congressmen and thousands of veterans rejected the board's findings.

What turned the tide of public opinion was unexpected and unpredictable. General Grant enlisted in Porter's army. Grant had done nothing for Porter in his various roles as General, General of the Army, Secretary of War, and President for two terms—as Eisenschiml reported, "Frank Hall, editor of the *Denver Post*, and one of Grant's friends, recalled that his wife also once had urged the President to take a more charitable view of General Porter, and received the brusque reply that Porter ought to have been shot." Approaching Grant by water, Porter used Admiral David Dixon Porter. The admiral, a proud part of the naval branch of the "Fighting Porters," who had directed the amphibious part of Grant's siege of Vicksburg, got his cousin an hour with Grant. Grant promised Porter only to review his papers and maps, some new and some going back to the war. After three days of review, Grant found himself, incredibly, like Choate, changing his mind about Porter.

Being convinced that Porter had done his duty, Grant acted. He hastily penned a short essay around Theodore Lord's schematic map of the August 29 positions of the armies at Second Bull Run. Despite Grant's misgivings that it was too rough to be published, his article, "An Undeserved Stigma," ran in the country's most widely-distributed magazine, the *North American Review*, in November, 1882. Grant declared that Porter had done his duty at Second Bull Run. As a result, the tablet on the front of Porter's monument states in large type after the Schofield board's members' names, that "their Judgment was approved by GENERAL U.S. GRANT."

Porter had written to his wife just after receiving the court-martial's guilty verdict, "I fear not the judgment of the court. I can proudly carry my head, and place my hand on my heart, and declare I never have done anything for which my country has reason for regret." He cast Grant's opinion in a similar way, phrasing it as Grant's belief that Porter "had committed no act, intentional or unintentional, by accident or oversight, by thought or word or deed, for which he was amenable to censure." It was enough. He had done nothing wrong and General Grant thought so, too. Not *facts* but his *state of mind* or *purity of heart* were Porter's focus after the court-martial, after Grant's article, and in his monument.

Porter finally understood. He had to "fail" Pope! He could never have obeyed the order to charge without both his own destruction and,

likely, that of Pope's army as well. A man ever ready to swear, his head
bared to his Creator, his hat over his heart, that *he had done nothing that
his country had any reason to regret*, Porter wrote, with evidence to believe
it, that "Longstreet was in my front with more than double my force, and
he has stated since the close of the war that my action not only saved our
army great loss and defeat, but in all probability saved the entire army
of General Pope." Porter circulated news of Grant's expert opinion even
more widely than he had the Schofield board's findings. Writing to Lincoln's surrogates, his wartime secretaries Nicolay and Hay, Porter used
the vocabulary of a saved soul. Porter asked the co-authors of the best-
selling multi-volume Lincoln biography to concur with Grant. He wrote
them that Grant

> had placed himself upon record unmistakably and
> unequivocally as antagonistic to me, induced to that
> course by the statements of my accuser who, at that time
> he believed to be reliable. Notwithstanding the position he
> had taken, he, after a careful personal examination of my
> case, with a moral courage almost sublime under the cir-
> cumstances, publicly and most decidedly exonerated me
> from all blame, and proclaimed that, in his opinion, I had
> committed no act, intentional or unintentional, by accident
> or oversight, by thought or word or deed, for which I was
> amenable to censure. Not only this, but he approved and
> justified my dispatches to Gen. Burnside, for which you
> malign me. This action of General Grant was one of the
> rarest in history. Need you hesitate to place yourself by
> the side of Gen. Grant, who has a grander history than any
> one man of this generation?

Porter's letter did no good. Married to their original opinion, Lincoln's opinion, Nicolay and Hay did not close ranks with Grant.

Porter was completely right about Grant's opinion. Grant was
an emphatic convert. Schofield saw Grant soon after "An Undeserved
Stigma" had been published and said that the enthusiastic Grant

> at once introduced the subject, and talked about it for a
> long time in the most earnest manner that I ever heard him
> speak on any subject. He would not permit me to utter a

single sentence until he had gone all over the case. He intimated very decidedly that no impartial and intelligent military man could, in his opinion, possibly reach any other conclusion than the one the board reached.

If, then, Second Bull Run is where Porter fought his "good fight," then Porter's 10,000 men were living monuments commemorating the general's moral decision. Kelly, guided by Porter, showed no fallen Union soldiers on his monument. That omission is clearly the moral intended by one of the most involuntarily enigmatic generals of the Civil War, Fitz John Porter.

10

Porter's Secret

Porter spoke his secret aloud only once.

Because Choate never wanted Porter to testify, Porter's attested admission was the worst problem Choate had to deal with before the Schofield board. William Blair Lord, a Congressional stenographer, a specialist in the art of transcription for over twenty years, the stenographer at Porter's court-martial, testified that he heard Porter say, "I was not true to Pope and there is no use denying it."

The best of all possible witnesses, a verbatim transcriber of words that he heard others speak, without any stake in the military generally or in the Bull Run controversy in particular, Lord was the perfect witness: a witness who had no reason to say that Porter said that except one—that Porter said it.

During the court-martial, Porter, under orders not to leave the city, rented rooms in Washington. At the end of one busy day, Lord, went to Porter's lodgings to retrieve documentary exhibits, telegrams that Porter had been lent to copy. Lord, essentially as an inadvertent eavesdropper, overheard Porter, still excited from that day's witnesses, talking to himself:

"I was not true to Pope and there is no use denying it."

This was dynamite, a virtual confession by the man on trial, but Lord only told the prosecutor about it after the record closed. After Lord testified, a trial lawyer for Porter would normally put Porter on the stand to deny it.

Choate did no such thing.

It seems that Choate could not.

He only cross-examined Lord, who stood his ground.

Lord had even written his wife at the time of the court-martial, a copy of which he read aloud from his letterpress:

"I have been a little bothered about General Fitz-John Porter. I had to go to his room on Monday to get some papers that belonged to the court that he had had to copy. While in the room, after some conversation, General Porter made the remark, 'Well, I wasn't loyal to Pope; there is no denying that.' Now, that is really the charge against him before the court-martial—that he did not do his duty as an officer before the enemy, and that he did not act rightly towards General Pope, his commanding officer. General Porter said what he did in the privacy of his own room; without thinking of the effect of his words. After thinking it over, I have concluded it better not to say anything about it now."

Worse for Choate and Porter, Lord had not been alone. A *New York Times* reporter, William Ormsby, had been present. Ormsby recalled similarly, though not identically, that Porter had said, "I warn't loyal to Pope, I was loyal to McClellan." Were both Lord and Ormsby lying?

When Choate argued in closing before the Schofield board, Choate did not suggest that the men were lying. He argued that Porter was excited during the trial and "had cause for immense excitement."

"He is a very cool man," Choate said, an understatement, "but do you question that his blood must have been up and that all there was in him of indignation and rage was stirred to its utmost depths?"

Choate discounted the remark as "an exclamation, excited and wrathful," a repudiation of the idea rather than a confession.

"I will not dwell on it," Choate said.

Neither did the Schofield board dwell on it. With new maps and Confederate witnesses, the three generals saw plainly that Porter would have been slaughtered had he charged when ordered to charge by Pope, or at any time during that afternoon. Porter was right to "not be true to Pope." He thus saved his men and—they saw clearly—Pope's army. In their report, the members of the Schofield board held unanimously that Porter had a positive duty to "fail" Pope. They said that they would not have held Porter "blameless for the fruitless sacrifice of his troops" on August 29, had he charged. The generals pointed to "a well-established military maxim that a corps commander is not justifiable in making an apparently hopeless attack in obedience to an order from a superior who is not on the spot, and who is evidently in error in respect to the essential conditions upon which the order is based."

The board made a finding that "an attack by Porter alone could have been but an ineffective blow, destructive only to the force that made it, and, followed by a counter-attack, disastrous to the Union army. Such an attack, under such circumstances, would have been not only a great blunder, but, on the part of an intelligent officer, it would have been a great crime."

The *great crime?* That would have been *murder*, the crime alleged against Lee by General Hill, observing the charge at Malvern Hill.

The maxim remains fresh. Today's official *Army Officer's Guide* talks about a country (Austria-Hungary) where a certain medal was awarded "to officers who, by *disobeying orders*, turned the tide and won important battles. In the U.S. Army, of course, there is no such medal; this sort of judgment, wrapped within a full, disciplined understanding of the legal and moral impact of decisions, is expected. It is the essence of the U.S. Army officer corps."

The board unanimously held that Porter "saved the Union army from disaster on the 29th of August." In other words, Porter did not turn the tide or win the Second Battle of Bull Run, but he did save the Army. Ironically, it was Lee who had shocked Porter into wariness of charging at Second Bull Run. It was Lee's waves of useless human sacrifices at Malvern Hill that Porter, walking through the gory dead and hearing cries of the wounded and dying there, took to heart. On the monument, as it was in Porter's memoir, the aftermath of Malvern Hill is sanitized enough not to be too graphic. A viewer moving chronologically from Malvern Hill to the front panel, where Porter's refusal to follow Lee is implicit, moves through what Porter moved through. Malvern Hill overshadows Second Bull Run on the monument as it did in Porter's life.

On the front panel, a line which like a saber stroke interrupts Porter's career, "CASHIERED JAN. 21st, 1863." With admirable ingenuity, Kelly shrank Porter's long exile from the military to its first day. In fact, the Schofield board recommended Porter's exoneration in 1879, Grant wrote his short essay, "An Undeserved Stigma" in late 1882, President Grover Cleveland signed Porter's relief act in mid-1886. Kelly skipped quickly to exoneration. Porter's exoneration pops up on his monument almost instantly. Arranged in the contours of a funeral urn, subtly suggesting the shape of many deaths avoided, the narrative reads:

ON THIS SITE
WAS BORN
FITZ JOHN PORTER
AUG. 31, 1822
WHILE HIS FATHER
CAPT. JOHN PORTER, U.S.N.
COMMANDED THE PORTSMOUTH NAVY YARD.
GRADUATED FROM WEST POINT, JULY 1845
DISTINGUISHED HIMSELF AND WAS WOUNDED IN WAR
WITH MEXICO
1846-1847.
INSTRUCTOR OF ARTILLERY AND CAVALRY
WEST POINT 1854-1855.
ASST. ADJ.GEN., UTAH EXPEDITION, 1857.
DURING CIVIL WAR
BREV. BRIG. GEN. U.S.A. JUNE 27, 1862
MAJ. GEN., U.S. VOL. JULY 4, 1862
COMMANDED 5TH ARMY CORPS.
CASHIERED JAN. 21ST, 1863
THE CASE OF GEN. PORTER WAS REVIEWED BY
A BOARD OF OFFICERS APPOINTED BY
PRESIDENT HAYES
CONSISTING OF
LIEUT. GEN. J.M. SCHOFIELD
BREV. MAJ. GEN. A.H. TERRY
BREV. MAJ. GEN. G.W. GETTY
HON. JOSEPH H. CHOATE COUNSEL FOR GEN. PORTER
THE BOARD FULLY EXONERATED HIM.
THEIR JUDGMENT WAS APPROVED BY
GENERAL U.S. GRANT.
FINALLY BY BOTH HOUSES OF CONGRESS
HE WAS RESTORED TO HIS FORMER
RANK IN THE REGULAR ARMY
BY
PRESIDENT CLEVELAND
DIED AT MORRISTOWN, NEW JERSEY
MAY 21ST, 1901

When his cousin funded a Northern shrine to keep Porter's memory alive, Porter and Kelly decided which of Porter's memories would be preserved. Images of the passive, suffering soldier are consistently Porter's and Kelly's choices. All moments commemorated are moments of reaction rather than action because Porter saved lives by inaction. The monument starts at the top with a seated man, no bullets flying, no battle raging, his horse arrested in mid-step as Porter literally "passes in review" before the visitors to Haven Park. Gallant Porter galloping on the night of July 1 to beg McClellan to attack Richmond the next day is not the statue that Porter and Kelly chose. Similarly, the wounded man falling is caught at the moment of going down. Porter, forced to hit the ground, is displayed rather than the bravest of one-man armies actively loading and firing before the Belén Gate. Porter without control in a runaway balloon, isolated and disconnected from events on the ground, is pictured rather than Porter the acrobat saving himself by climbing ropes to pull the gas cord. Even the most warlike panel, Malvern Hill, is static. The battle is over, dead and wounded rebels lie at Porter's feet while he rides with no obvious connection to them or to any ongoing battle. It is a scene of no shots, no artillery, no gun smoke, rather than Porter in the thick of the action, repelling Lee's charges. Even the words on the fourth panel, at the front of the monument, are passive. Behind Porter "cashiered" and then "exonerated" in a report that was "approved" by General Grant is the shuffle of papers distant from the hurly-burly of combat, bloodshed and the cannon's blasts. Cautious Porter who reacted and defended is presented, not Porter dispatching couriers, riding, sword in hand, and giving orders in the middle of Second Bull Run. Porter helped Kelly to design a monument that would honor his secret decision to "fail Pope" by *not* following the example of Lee at Malvern Hill.

After Second Bull Run, Porter ironically and poignantly held the limited war line in front of and contrary to his military ideal and friend, General McClellan. President Lincoln had asked McClellan to take charge again while Pope had been hustled back to the West to fight Indians. Porter was standing on the spot, *déjà vu*, as Lee's invasion of Maryland ended. When McClellan threw Union troops at Lee at Antietam in mid-September, 1862, Porter stood at his side. Mac's ambition overwhelmed his habitual caution. During the battle, McClellan yelled his intention to "wipe out the memory of Bull Run." No longer the paradigm of limited warfare, a Napoleonic "Little Mac" ordered Burnside into repeated charges to take a bridge "if it takes 10,000 men." The number was eerie. Only the previous month at Second Bull Run, Porter had protected 10,000 men from dying in a reckless charge. At Antietam, McClellan presided over the bloodiest single day battle in American history. Hesitating to stop as the sun set, Mac looked at Porter. George Smalley of the *New York Tribune* reported his observations at that critical moment:

> McClellan's glass for the last half-hour has seldom been turned away from the left. He sees clearly enough that Burnside is pressed- needs no messenger to tell him that. His face grows darker with anxious thought, turns a half-questioning look on Fitz-John Porter, who stands by his side, gravely scanning the field. But Porter slowly shakes his head and one may believe that the same thought is passing through the minds of both generals. "They are the only reserves of the army; they cannot be spared."

Long after the war, Porter told Kelly, "I consider the Battle of Antietam was the turning-point of the whole contest. It showed that Lee could be licked." But on the scene Porter literally shook his head. His mentor McClellan had, at Antietam, replicated Malvern Hill before his eyes. As usual, Porter spoke aloud no criticism of McClellan. The disgust he felt he projected onto Lincoln. Two weeks after Antietam, Porter wrote a New York editor that the Emancipation Proclamation would "tend only to prolong the war by rousing bitter feelings of the south, and causing unity of action among them, while the reverse with us. Those who fight the battles of the country wish to see the war ended honorably—by a restoration of the Union, not merely by a suppression of the rebellion, for there is a wide difference." Disturbed by Lincoln's policy change and shaking his head at McClellan's change in tactics, Porter began to consider resigning from the Army. Ironically, the Army first cashiered Porter, who spent most of the rest of his life trying to get reinstated. At Porter's exoneration trial, his advocate, Joseph Choate, ironically raised bloody Antietam in Porter's defense.

In almost his last words to the Schofield board, Choate asked about Porter, "If he was a sacrifice to discipline, has it not answered its purpose? If it was necessary to strike down an innocent man to enforce discipline upon suspected men in the Army of the Potomac, has it not done its work? Look at them under all commanders, before and certainly

Porter was near McClellan at the end of the bloodiest single day in the history of American arms, Antietam, September 17, 1862. He shook his head. On that day, McClellan, vowing expressly to wipe out the memory of Bull Run, ordered Union troops under Burnside to take a bridge "if it takes 10,000 men." This kind of equation made no sense to Porter nor had it made sense earlier in the war to McClellan. At that time, President Lincoln, shown meeting with McClellan and his corps commanders after the battle, had only kind words for Porter, who stands second, after the chair, behind Lincoln. (Photo courtesy of the Library of Congress; James Erik, http:// JamesErik.com.)

afterwards—look at them from Antietam to the last struggles in the Wilderness, under the successive commands of McClellan, Burnside, Hooker, Meade and Grant. When, anywhere, did a man of them fail to do his whole duty?"

Porter, sitting solemnly beside his august counsel, had to sit in silence while Choate praised McClellan at Antietam, Burnside at Fredericksburg, Hooker at Chancellorsville, Meade at Gettysburg and Grant in several battles, ending with Petersburg, all instances of war by attrition when Union generals followed the mindset of Lee at Malvern Hill, the line that Porter refused to cross. Unlike Choate's final argument, and quite beyond the Schofield board's conclusions, Kelly's monument combines a condemnation of Lee by displaying the sorry results of his repeated charges at Malvern Hill with Grant's approval of Porter's inaction on August 29, 1862 as having been the right tactic.

In May 1901, at Porter's funeral, where Kelly was a pall-bearer, Kelly met General John Schofield. A week later, the general who had presided over Porter's second hearing sat in a Manhattan studio to have Kelly draw his portrait. Schofield had written his memoirs. In them, he described General Porter's visit to the War Department in 1868 about a possible appeal. His account had been plain vanilla. Sitting before Kelly, Schofield dropped his public pose.

Unknown until published in William Styple's book in 2005, Schofield told Kelly that he had specifically spelled out to Porter, "You must be prepared to prove, not that you did what in your judgment was best, but you must be prepared to prove that you literally carried out the orders of Pope. In the first trial, the fact that you did what was best would be accepted as a proper excuse for not obeying Pope. But in the second trial, in passing on the judgment of the first, you have got to prove that you carried out the orders of Pope to the letter, without asserting your own." Accordingly, when Porter appeared before the man who gave him those instructions, he did not testify. His lawyer, Joseph Choate, argued vigorously that Porter's attempt to obey Pope's orders was thwarted by physical impossibility. Porter won his case but his actual thoughts and disobedience on August 29, 1862 thus remained his secret. Accessible only after his death by inferences, Porter wove his secret into the monument that he and Kelly designed together. It is, finally, not history books or trial transcripts or reports of military boards but the monument that stands in Haven Park opposite his childhood home that embodies the history of Fitz John Porter—and tells the secret of his moral heroism at last.

Acknowledgments

The conclusions I draw here are my own. Readers will please not fault any author I quote or cite as being a proponent, let alone an originator, of my theory of Porter at Second Bull Run, or of his miserable childhood, or of his close bonding with his schoolmaster or of the meaning of his monument. Some of the authors to whom I owe most would certainly disagree with many, if not all, of the inferences I make of facts and quotations they offer. Among them, John J. Hennessy, who wrote a comprehensive book on Second Bull Run, the first in over a hundred years on this turning point of the Civil War, for which he deserves the country's gratitude, believes that Porter was a relatively poor performer or mediocre soldier. Through Styple's book, without which I would have been in no position to develop the Porter-Kelly relationship behind the monument, one meets Porter as a very mellow fellow indeed. Styple's book reveals that Porter spoke about Antietam as a good thing unconditionally, a turning point. I emphasize instead the Porter on the scene who shook his head at McClellan at the end of the most bloody day in the history of American arms. I researched and weighed sources listed in the Bibliography to discern that Porter's life, which I find to have been heroic, was a series of successes against the odds, in surviving childhood trauma to blossom into a reserved but brilliant young man, in getting into West Point, where he graduated near the top of his class, in living through the Mexican War, especially where others fell, at the Belén Gate, in making a military career in the east, west and the south, wherever assigned, in pitched battle or on secret assignment, in overcoming the deficiencies of primitive technology, taking the reins of a runaway balloon, becoming the most enthusiastic proponent of American air power up until Billy Mitchell, and, finally, in reclaiming his reputation against the greatest odds of all—by designing a monument to himself to be built in the center of his old hometown, Portsmouth, New Hampshire.

I want to thank Doug Kerr, photographer extraordinaire, the *sine qua non* of this book; James Erik, the fabulous researcher; the faculty of the University of Massachusetts Boston's History Department, who opened the past for me as my future; Manuel Simoes, always a help;

Deidre Randall, patient publisher, of Peter E. Randall Publisher, a New Hampshire institution.

Finally, I am grateful to Fitz John Porter for living a life so filled with exciting, colorful, dramatic and daring exploits against the odds. Now, some may still think that Fitz John Porter's life, as recounted here, is too good to be true and that I got it wrong. I suggest that any doubtful or curious reader follow the evidence. For that purpose, I append an extensive Bibliography.

About the Author

Wayne Soini has been interested in the Civil War since its centennial, when he was twelve years old. A 2009 graduate of the University of Massachusetts Boston's master's degree program in history, during which the author's draft thesis was on the topic presented here in a popular format, Soini here publishes his third book.

Bibliography

Newspapers
Boston Daily Globe
Boston Transcript

Periodicals
North American Review

Archival collections
Burnside Papers, Rhode Island Historical Society Research Library
Kelly Papers, New York Historical Society
Porter Papers, Library of Congress
Porter Papers, Massachusetts Historical Society
Ropes Papers, Howard Gotlieb Archival Research Center, Boston
      University
Suffolk County Probate Court Records, Massachusetts Archives

Books
Anders, Curt. *Injustice on Trial*. Zionsville, Indiana: Guild Press Emmis
      Publishing, L.P., 2002.
Anderson, Robert. *An Artillery Officer in the Mexican War, 1846-47*. New
      York: G.P. Putnam's Sons, 1911.
Anonymous. Biographical Sketch of Gen. Fitz-John Porter from
      Encyclopedia of Contemporary Biography. New York: Atlantic
      Publishing and Engraving Company, 1885.
Basler, Roy P., ed. *The Collected Works of Abraham Lincoln*. New
      Brunswick, N.J.: Rutgers University Press, 1953.
Brown, Harry James, and Frederick D. Williams, ed. *The Diary of James
      A. Garfield*. Michigan State University Press, 1981.
Cox, Jacob D. *The Second Battle of Bull Run as connected with the Fitz John
      Porter Case*. Cincinnati: Peter G. Thomson, 1882.
Cozzens, Paul, and Robert I. Girardi, ed. *The Military Memoirs of General
      John Pope*. Chapel Hill, N.C.: The University of North Carolina
      Press, 1998.
Davis, Donald A. *Stonewall Jackson*. New York: Palgrave Macmillan, 2007.

Dougherty, Kevin. *Civil War Leadership and Mexican War Experience.* Jackson, Mississippi: University Press of Mississippi, 2007.

Dowdey, Clifford. *The Seven Days: The Emergence of Robert E. Lee.* Boston: Little, Brown, 1964.

Eicher, David J. *The Civil War in Books: An Analytical Bibliography.* Urbana: University of Illinois Press, 1997.

Eisenschiml, Otto. O.E., *Historian without an Armchair.* New York: The Bobbs-Merrill Company, Inc., 1963.

_____. *The Celebrated Case of Fitz-John Porter.* New York: The Bobbs-Merrill Company, Inc., 1950.

Foote, Shelby. *The Civil War; A Narrative. Volume I, "Fort Sumter to Perryville,"* New York: Random House, 1958.

Fowler, Will. *Santa Anna of Mexico.* Lincoln: University of Nebraska Press, 2007.

Gabler, Henry. *The Fitz John Porter Case: Politics and Military Justice.* New York: Unpublished dissertation, City College of New York, 1979.

Grant, Ulysses S. *General Grant's Unpublished Correspondence in the Case of General Porter.* New York: Martin B. Brown, ca. 1885.

_____ *General Grant's Memoirs.* New York: Library of America, 1990.

Hattaway, Herman and Archer Jones. *How the North Won.* Urbana: University of Illinois Press, 1983.

Hennessy, John J. *Return to Bull Run, The Campaign and Battle of Second Manassas.* New York: Simon & Schuster, 1993.

Holzer, Harold, ed. *Lincoln's White House Secretary, The Adventurous Life of William O. Stoddard.* Carbondale, Illinois: Southern Illinois University Press, 2007.

Hubbell, John T., ed. *Battles Lost and Won, Essays from Civil War History.* Westport, Connecticut: Greenwood Press, 1975.

Jermann, Donald R. Fitz-John Porter, *Scapegoat of Second Manassas; The Rise, Fall and Rise of the General Accused of Disobedience.* Jefferson, North Carolina: McFarland & Company, Inc., 2009.

Johnson, Robert U., and Clarence C. Buel, eds. *Battles and Leaders of the Civil War.* 4 vols. New York: Century, 1887-1888.

Keegan, John. *The Face of Battle; A Study of Agincourt, Waterloo, and the First Day of the Somme.* New York: Viking, 1976.

Lee, Robert E. *Lee's Dispatches.* Ed. Douglas Southall Freeman. New York: 1957.

_____, *Wartime Papers of Robert E. Lee.* Ed. Clifford Dowdey and Louis H. Manarin. Boston: Little, Brown, 1961.

Long, David E. *Nothing Too Daring; A Biography of Commodore David Porter, 1780-1843.* Annapolis, Maryland: United States Naval Institute, 1970.

Lord, Theodore A. *A Summary of the Case of General Fitz-John Porter.* San Francisco: H.S. Crocker & Co., 1883.

Loving, Jerome M., ed. *The Civil War Letters of George Washington Whitman.* Durham, N.C.: Duke University Press, 1975.

Macnamara, Daniel George. *History of the 9th Regiment, Massachusetts Volunteer Infantry.* Boston: n.p., 1899.

Mansfield, Edward D. *The Mexican War; A History of Its Origin and A Detailed Account of the Victories which terminated in the Surrender of the Capital; With the Official Despatches of the Generals.* New York: A.S. Barnes & Co., 1849.

Mann, Thomas. *Fighting with the Eighteenth Massachusetts, The Civil War Memoir of Thomas H. Mann.* Ed. John J. Hennessy. Baton Rouge: Louisiana State University Press, 2000.

Albert Nelson Marquis, ed., *Who's Who in New England,* Chicago: Albert Nelson Marquis & Co.

Martin, Edward Sanford. *The Life of Joseph Hodges Choate As Gathered Chiefly from his Letters.* New York: Charles Scribner's Sons, 1921.

McClellan, George B. *McClellan's Own Story.* New York: Charles L. Webster & Company, 1887.

McPherson, James M. *Battle Cry of Freedom.* New York: Oxford University Press, 1988.

Moran, Philip R., ed. *Ulysses S. Grant, 1822-1885;* Chronology, Documents, Bibliographical Aids. New York: Oceana Publications, Inc., 1968.

Nevins, Allan. *The War for the Union, Vol. 2, "War Becomes Revolution."* New York: Charles Scribner's Sons, 1960.

Nicolay, Helen. *Lincoln's Secretary, A Biography of John G. Nicolay.* New York: Longmans, Green and Co., 1949.

Official Records, War of Rebellion; Official Records of the Union and Confederate Armies. Washington, D.C.: Government Printing Office, various years.

Porter, Fitz-John. *Letter to General J.D. Cox.* Morristown, N.J.: n.p., ca. 1880.

_____. *General Fitz John Porter's Reply to Hon. Zachariah Chandler's Speech in the U.S. Senate.* Morristown, N.J., n.p., ca. 1876.

_____. *Reply to the Rejoinder of Major General John Pope to the Appeal of Major General Fitz John Porter, for a Re-examination of the Proceedings of the Court-martial in his Case.* Morristown, N.J., n.p., 1870.

Proceedings and Report of the board of officers convened by Special Orders number 78, Headquarters of the Army, Washington, April 12, 1878, in the Case of Fitz John Porter, Washington: Government Printing Office, 1879.

Ropes, John C. *The Army Under Pope.* New York: Charles Scribner's Sons, 1881,

Ross, Charles D. *Acoustic Shadows.* Shippenburg, Pennsylvania: White Mane Books, 2001.

Schofield, John M. *Forty-Six Years in the Army.* Norman, Oklahoma: University of Oklahoma Press, 1998 reprint of 1889 edition.

Schutz, Wallace, and Walter N. Trenerry. *Abandoned by Lincoln.* Urbana: University of Illinois Press, 1990.

Sears, Stephen. Controversies & Commanders: *Dispatches from the Army of the Potomac.* Boston: Houghton Mifflin, 1992.

_____, ed. *Collected Correspondence of General George B. McClellan.* New York: Ticknor & Fields, 1989.

_____. *Young Napoleon.* New York: Ticknor & Fields, 1988.

Smith, George Winston, and Charles Judah. *Chronicles of the Gringoes; The U.S. Army in the Mexican War 1846-1848; Accounts of Eyewitnesses & Combatants.* Albuquerque, University of New Mexico, 1968.

Styple, William B., ed. *Generals in Bronze, Interviewing the Commanders of the Civil War.* Kearny, N.J.: Belle Grove Publishing Company, 2005.

Thayer, William Roscoe, ed. *The Life and Letters of John Hay.* Vol. II. Boston: Houghton Mifflin Company, 1908.

Webb, Alexander S. The Peninsula; *McClellan's Campaign of 1862.* New York: Charles Scribner's Sons, 1881.

Weld, Stephen Minot. *War Diary and Letters of Stephen Minot Weld, 1861-1865.* Boston: Massachusetts Historical Society, 1979.

Welles, Gideon, and Howard K. Beale, eds., assisted by Alan W. Brownsword. *Diary of Gideon Welles, Secretary of the Navy Under*

Lincoln and Johnson. 3 volumes. New York: W.W. Norton & Company, Inc., 1960.

Wilson, William Bender. *Acts and Actors in the Civil War*. Lancaster, Pennsylvania: The New Era Print, 1892.

Worthington, Thomas. *A Correct History of Pope, McDowell and Fitz John Porter at the Second Battle of Bull Run, August 29, 1862*. Washington: Thomas McGill & Co., 1880.

Wylie, Paul R. *The Irish General; Thomas Francis Meagher*. Norman, Oklahoma: University of Oklahoma Press, 2007.

Index